PERU

TITLES IN THE MODERN NATIONS OF THE WORLD SERIES INCLUDE:

Austria
Brazil
Canada
China
Cuba
Egypt
England
Ethiopia
Germany
Greece
Haiti
India
Ireland
Italy
Japan
Jordan
Kenya
Mexico
Norway
Poland
Russia
Saudi Arabia
Scotland
Somalia
South Africa
South Korea
Spain
Sweden
Switzerland
Taiwan
The United States
Vietnam

PERU

BY LAUREL CORONA

LUCENT BOOKS
P.O. BOX 289011
SAN DIEGO, CA 92198-9011

On Cover: Street scene, Cuzco, Peru.

Library of Congress Cataloging-in-Publication Data

Corona, Laurel, 1949–
    Peru / by Laurel Corona.
        p.   cm. — (Modern nations of the world)
    Includes bibliographical references and index.
    Summary: Examines the land, people and history of Peru and discusses
its current state of affairs and place in the world today.
    ISBN 1-56006-862-0 (alk. paper)
    1. Peru—Juvenile literature. I. Title.   II. Series.
  F3408.5 .C67 2001
  985—dc21   00-012188

CONTENTS

INTRODUCTION

A PAUPER ON A THRONE OF GOLD

Peruvians often call their country "*el pais de las maravillas*" (the country of marvels). The nickname is a good one, for this country is truly marvelous geographically, culturally, and historically. Here, at the eastern edge of the spectacular Andes mountains, water collects to form the Amazon Basin. Here, the rock walls of mysterious cultures emerge from the sides of mountains, and ceremonial platforms and tombs lie buried under the dust and vegetation of centuries. Here, the beauty and richness visible to the eye give rise to curiosity about how much still remains unseen and undiscovered.

There is always more than meets the eye in Peru, always something to keep one guessing. Amateur archaeologist and explorer Hiram Bingham learned this in 1911, when, looking for something else, he stumbled across Machu Picchu, a stunning Inca city high on a mountaintop in the Andes. Believing he had found another lost city, Vilcabamba, the last refuge of powerful inhabitants known as Inca before their fall to the Spanish *conquistadores* in the sixteenth century, Bingham never realized he was looking in the wrong place altogether. Only recently has it been clearly established that the lost city of Vilcabamba is far away in the jungles of the Amazon.

BRIGHT COLORS, GRIM REALITIES

Visitors to Peru are often dazzled, as Hiram Bingham was, by the astonishing natural beauty and awe-inspiring historical sites that residents often seem simply too busy to notice. But Peruvians do indeed pay great attention to beauty, as shown by the bright woven patterns of their ethnic costumes and the beautifully decorated objects in their daily lives. In fact, the most indelible impressions of Peru usually involve elements of both natural beauty and colorful human cultures. In a highland marketplace, people in brightly striped and patterned skirts and shawls, their braids dropping below their traditional brimmed hats, sell their wares against the backdrop of jagged, snow-covered peaks. In the Amazon Basin along the border with Brazil, a jungle clearing explodes with the sounds and colors of tropical birds investigating the activities of the people going about their daily lives. Along the coast, amid the muffled roar of waves breaking on a nearby beach, graceful fishing boats woven from reeds move quietly in serene grassy lagoons.

Though Peru is one of the most beautiful countries on earth, it also has serious economic and social problems. The cheerful melodies of flutes and the bright patterned shawls worn by villagers lift the hearts of all who hear and see them in Andean marketplaces, but they mask the stark poverty of village life. Only those strong enough to survive childhood without succumbing to diseases easily prevented where better health care is available ever hear the flutes or wear the shawls. Those who by necessity or by ambition leave their homes in the Amazon or the Andes to try their luck in the cities of Lima, Arequipa, or Trujillo find levels of degradation they could not even have imagined. Half of Lima's residents live in shantytowns erected seemingly overnight from whatever materials are at hand. People live without running water or electricity and with little pro-

These women, about to enter an open-air market, wear clothing typical of villagers across Peru.

tection from the elements. They survive by relying on one another, bringing their traditions of community effort and mutual concern with them.

Many, in fact, still feel better off even under these abject conditions than they did at home, especially those who fled in the 1980s and early 1990s from groups such as Sendero Luminoso, or Shining Path, who terrorized the countryside in the name of political revolution. Others have fled from the lawlessness caused by massive drug trafficking in coca, the source of cocaine, which dominates the economy of the eastern slopes of the Andes and many, always poor, found themselves even poorer as a result of environmental disasters. Some of these are natural, such as the flooding, earthquakes, and massive landslides common to Peru and some are caused by humans, such as the damage done to the rain forest by mining and other efforts to make a profit from the vast natural resources of Peru.

"Todos las Sangres"

Culturally and ethnically, the people of Peru have mingled their Andean and Amazonian blood with that of Europeans, Africans, and Asians to the extent that they could be fairly said to have "*todos las sangres*," or "all the bloods," the title of a novel by Peruvian author José María Arguedas. This ethnic diversity has created a unique, vibrant, and colorful culture. The world became aware of this fact when Alberto Fujimori, son of Japanese immigrants, became president of the country in 1990. However, the dozens of labels, many derogatory, used to describe exactly how dark or light skinned one is; how much European, Andean, African, or other ancestry one can claim; and how much money one makes, are evidence that though the people of Peru may be ethnically mixed, the culture is far from a melting pot. Though a dark-skinned family will be accepted in the highest levels of society without apparent prejudice if they have managed to become rich, it is nevertheless clear that the darker the skin, the more likely a person is to be poor, and the fewer chances he or she will have of breaking loose from poverty.

Ethnic mingling still mainly occurs in the major population centers. Many of the Andean Indians, descendants of the Inca, still live much as they have for centuries. Anthropologists believe that there may be groups living in the Amazon who have never had contact with the outside world, and there are a number of groups with whom only fleeting contact has ever

Despite Peru's vast resources and potential for growth, most Peruvians struggle with poverty.

been established. Centuries of evidence shows that indigenous cultures are usually destroyed or at least badly weakened by contact with the outside world, as the Inca were by the Spanish. Because of this fact, indigenous people are at the least cautious and wary about interaction with outsiders and often resist it aggressively, even to the point of violence. But the world will not stay away, especially when the lands that indigenous people occupy are rich in mineral, agricultural, or other sources of wealth. Therefore, one of the main issues in today's Peru is how to create a unified nation when so many of its people perceive themselves as having more to lose than to gain by being part of it.

A Pauper on a Throne of Gold

According to Library of Congress researcher and editor Rex A. Hudson, "Although Peru is endowed with perhaps the widest range of resources in South America, somehow they have never been coherently or effectively utilized to construct a balanced and progressive society."[1] The problem is an economic as well as a social one. The poverty of the vast majority of Peruvians has resulted in the growth of a day-to-day culture based around simple survival and the support networks necessary for that end. Who is president and how much power that office holds, whether the country is socialist or capitalist, and what sorts of policies and laws are in effect make little difference to the Andean peasant as he sips his cup of *mate* before going to dig in his fields. It makes little difference to the young girl who sweeps the dust from the entryway of a house in anticipation of its occupants' return from a vacation to Disney World or Paris. It makes little difference to the Ashaninka family who tries (and perhaps fails) to keep their children from harm at the hands of terrorists or drug traffickers, the true rulers of many Amazon communities.

Yet many Peruvians have not given up hope that there may be a governmental solution to the economic and social problems that grip this nation. It is a land extraordinarily rich in natural resources, including any country's greatest resource—its people. As Hudson writes, "The irony of Peru's condition was captured long ago in the characterization of the nation as being a 'pauper sitting on a throne of gold.' How to put the gold in the pauper's pockets without destroying the chair on which to sit is a puzzle that Peruvians and their international supporters have yet to solve."[2] If the government could increase people's confidence that greater participation in the political, social, and economic life of Peru would improve their lives, and then deliver on the promises it made, the twenty-first century could see a powerful resurgence of this nation, one that would make the Inca proud.

1

The Many Colors of Peru

The geography of Peru not only contributes to its great beauty, but is one of its greatest assets because it supports a wealth of natural resources. However, the difficult terrain of the Amazon and Andes has also served to isolate many of Peru's people, and even today the people of Peru's interior have little in common with those who live on the narrow and heavily populated coastal strip. The land itself, therefore, is clearly one of the major influences on Peruvian culture and history, as well as a critical factor in its economy and social structure.

The Northern Coast

A narrow strip of desert stretches the full length of coastal Peru. Near sea level, sand dunes are held in place by hardy vegetation, and where the elevation rises, the rocky and deeply eroded land is home to cactus and other drought-resistant plant life. However, because of the capability of irrigating at least parts of this region with rivers created by runoff from snow and rain in the mountains to the east, significant stretches of the coast have not been left in this dry and unproductive state. Long before the Inca Empire, wherever small rivers crossed valleys, farmers created ways of irrigating fields, and thus for several millennia this naturally dry region has been a center for agriculture.

The northernmost stretches of the Peruvian coast lie in the provinces of Tumbes, Piura, and Lambayeque. Tumbes's principal town, also named Tumbes, is less than twenty miles from the border with Ecuador and was the first Inca settlement that Spanish explorer Francisco Pizarro saw. The region's white beaches where he first landed are today lined with small sailboats used for fishing, a major source of income. A little farther south lies the province of Piura and its principal towns, Piura and Talara. Talara is the center of a petroleum-producing region. A desert oasis community, it is also close to both the well-known deep-sea fishing center of Cabo Blanco, a favorite of fabled sportsman and writer Ernest Hemingway, and a famous surfing beach at nearby Mancora, where many international competitions are held. Though sports draw many visitors here, Peruvians often make a point of traveling to this remote part of the country for another reason—to seek the advice of the *brujos* (witches), healers, and fortune-tellers for which the region is known.

South of Piura is the province of Lambayeque, home to the coastal city of Chiclayo. "This bustling city," explains author Pam Barrett, "is a major commercial hub for northern Peru and is a lively and friendly spot with few pretensions."[3] Like its neighboring communities to the north, Chiclayo is a hub for faith healers and practitioners of traditional medicines. Its Mercado

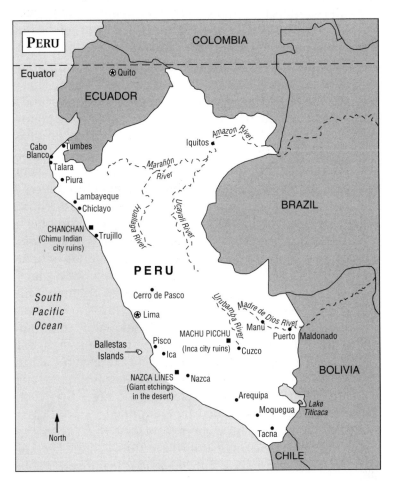

de Brujos (Witchcraft Market) is one of the largest and best known in South America. Chiclayo is also a jumping-off point for the ruins at nearby Sipán and Tucume. At Tucume a cluster of twenty-six adobe pyramids offer a tantalizing glimpse of the still mysterious pre-Inca culture of the Moche people.

THE CENTRAL COAST

The provinces of La Libertad, Ancash, and Callao lie along the central coast of Peru. This coastal region contains some of the country's best agricultural land, and it is also well known for its many archaeological sites, particularly the ancient cities of Chan Chan and Sechin.

La Libertad is best known as the location of Trujillo, which with its 1.2 million population is the second largest city in Peru. Named after Pizarro's hometown in Spain, it grew as an important port of call for the Spanish on the long trip between Lima and Quito, Ecuador. Trujillo's showcase is the Plaza de las Armas, a beautifully maintained square of colonial buildings, a cathedral, and other landmarks, where "one can see the comings and goings of the city's elderly men who stake out shady benches to read their morning newspapers, the young mothers carrying their market baskets, with toddlers in tow, or uniformed schoolgirls huddled together sharing secrets."[4] Trujillo, according to author Dilwyn Jenkins, "looks every bit the oasis it is, standing in a relatively green irrigated valley bounded by arid desert at the foot of the Andes. It hardly seems a city of a million inhabitants—walk twenty minutes in any direction and you're out in open fields, hedged by flowering shrubs."[5]

Lima, farther south at the almost exact center of the Peruvian coast, is the country's capital and most important city. Almost a third of Peru's population lives in Lima and its suburbs. As writer Jane Holligan de Diaz-Limaco explains, "Lima is a city which has burst its banks, which is out of control, a city where the anarchy born of poverty is on every sidewalk."[6] In the last fifty years, Lima has grown from under 2 million to close to 8 million. Much of this growth is because, for the first time in history, Andean people are leaving their home communities and going to Lima to escape rural violence or simply to find a way to make money.

Lima is unable to house its population, and shantytowns set up on the sand dunes on the outskirts of town often become permanent communities with miserable living conditions.

However, despite all its problems, there is a charm to Lima. Scattered throughout the city are the remains of Inca and pre-Inca shrines and beautiful colonial buildings. East of the city, upscale residential communities for Lima's most affluent residents include private swimming pools and lush gardens, as well as golf courses, tennis clubs, and other amenities. But regardless of where and how one lives, residents of Lima all must endure the gloomy weather that pervades the Lima area much of the year. An atmospheric condition called thermal inversion produces gray skies and heavy damp air, a condition called the *garua*, for months at a time.

THE SOUTHERN COAST

The provinces of Ica, Arequipa, Moquegua, and Tacna make up the southern coast. One of the region's most significant sights is the Paracas Natural Reserve near Pisco. Paracas means "raining sand" in Quechua, the Inca language, an apt name because the area is subject to high winds that blow astonishing

Lima, with a population of almost 8 million, is Peru's capital and most important city.

quantities of sand. Dolphins, seals, and orcas are found in the bay, and condors and other exotic animals search for food on land. Off the coast are the Ballestas Islands, sometimes called the Guano Islands because they are covered with guano, or bird droppings, once of great value as fertilizer.

Slightly inland from the southern coast is the city of Ica, a center of wine production. Founded in 1543 by Pizarro, Ica was moved several times because earthquakes destroyed the first few locations. It is home to one of the best archaeological museums in the country, which includes an outstanding collection of ancient textiles and ceramics as well as models of the Nazca Lines, ancient carvings that are located nearby. Another inland city of interest is Arequipa, which according to legend got its name from the Inca emperor Mayta Capac saying "*ari quepay*," which means roughly "Okay—let's stop here."[7]

La Montaña

On the other side of Peru lies the region known as *la selva*. Twice the size of the rest of the country, it includes the tropical rain forest of the Amazon Basin (the low *selva*) and the eastern mountain slopes of the Andes, which are called *la montaña*, or the high *selva*. It was such a forbidding barrier to the Spanish that the last Inca were able to escape and live in *la montaña* for many years before their final defeat. Legends still abound about hidden treasures they were supposed to have taken and left in the high *selva*.

The high *selva* runs the length of Peru's eastern mountains. Nicknamed "*la ceja de selva*" (the eyebrow of the selva), much of the region is what is known as a cloud forest—a densely vegetated area almost always draped in mist and clouds. The eastern Andes drop off quickly to the flat plain of the Amazon Basin below, and the torrential waters of the Marañón, Apurímac, Huallaga, and Urubamba Rivers are a major feature of the terrain. In recent years efforts have been made to turn land in the "eyebrow" into commercially profitable farms and to harvest more heavily its valuable cedar and mahogany forests. The illegal cultivation of coca sent to Colombia and other countries for processing into cocaine has also increased. These activities have been undertaken without concern for the environmental impact on the Amazon Basin, and pesticide runoff and erosion are increasing problems for the lands farther downstream.

THE RAIN FOREST

Most people who view the rain forests of the world see them from one of two perspectives. From the air, rain forests look—in the words of Pam Barrett, author and editor of *Insight Guide: Peru*—"like an endless sea of lumpy green sponges." From the ground, one looks up through vegetation so thick that 95 percent of the light from above is blocked out. In fact, contrary to the popular image of people hacking through undergrowth and getting tangled up in vines, the forest floor is actually quite bare because there is too little light for most ground cover to take hold.

But, as Barrett points out, the rain forest contains many other environments between the treetops and the jungle floor. "If you were able to enter the upper canopy slowly from the top you would discover that the first layer is virtually a desert," as a result of the burning sun and often high winds that evaporate moisture. Many of the plants, called epiphytes, which live in the notches of rain forest tree branches, are actually cactuslike. Lower down in the canopy, where there is a little more protection from sun and wind, vegetation is lush. It becomes sparse again as light dims closer to the ground.

According to Barrett,

It is this enormous variation of light, wind, and temperature that, together with the thousands of different species of plants, affords a million different homes for animal and plant species. Whole communities of insects, birds, and other animals are specialized and adapted to different levels of the rainforest, so it is not surprising that it contains the highest species diversity in the world.

For example, there are twelve hundred known species of butterfly in the Peruvian rain forest (and likely many more will be discovered in the future) and only four hundred on the entire continent of Europe.

THE NORTHERN LOW *SELVA*

The low *selva* is divided into two distinct regions, one in the north and one in the south of the country. In both regions thousands of square miles of thick rain forest are broken only by meandering rivers and lakes. The northern *selva*, known administratively as the province of Loreto, is where the runoff from the eastern Andes collects and forms the initial stretch of the Amazon River.

The diversity of plant and animal life in this region, as well as in the high *selva*, is astonishing. Literally millions of species of animals, from insects to large predators such as jaguars, pythons, and caiman, live in the low *selva*. Other well-known animal species include piranha, wild parrots, and innumerable varieties of monkeys, birds, butterflies, and snakes. Biologists are confident there are still millions of species—particularly of smaller animals such as fish and insects, as well as many plant species—that have not yet been identified.

Few villages are noteworthy enough to show on general maps of the region. In the innumerable small villages not on the map, people live by fishing, collecting food from the jungle, growing small crops, and trading with neighboring villages. Many indigenous groups are suspicious of outsiders, and stereotypical images of poison dart guns wielded against strangers by naked but fantastically adorned locals are not entirely off the mark in parts of the low *selva*.

IQUITOS

The only population center large enough to be on any map of the northern Amazon region is Iquitos. It seems almost impossible that a city of 400,000 people could exist in the middle of deep jungle, connected to the outside world by not even a single road. All travel to and from Iquitos is by air or riverboat. In fact, Iquitos probably would never have been more than a sleepy small village were it not for the rubber boom at the turn of the twentieth century. When a means was developed to turn the latex from rubber trees into a substance hard enough to make tires and other useful objects, Iquitos became a center of the rubber trade; and for a brief few decades, it was one of the busiest and wealthiest cities on earth. "Rubber barons" decorated their lavish homes, some of which can still be viewed today, with intricate ironwork, beautiful tiles, and elaborate chandeliers.

Today the most vibrant and interesting part of Iquitos is Belen, a community of houses and businesses built on rafts that float on canals. As writer Barrett describes it, "Belen is the center for an incredible variety of Amazon products: exotic fruits, fish, turtles, edible frogs, herbal medicines and water fowl. Plowing the water ways are . . . canoe-taxis paddled by Iquitenos [residents of Iquitos], some as young as five years old."[8] The economy of Iquitos today is assisted by its role as a center of tourism. People wanting to visit the Amazon often fly to Iquitos, then continue by riverboat into the deep jungle.

THE SOUTHERN LOW *SELVA*

The rain forest region at the southern end of Peru, in the provinces of Ucayali and Madre de Dios, is "one of the truly pristine areas of the tropics."[9] Its major rivers, the Urubamba

MACHU PICCHU

Machu Picchu, one of the fabled cities of the Inca and one of the most easily recognizable landmarks in Peru today, was not known to outsiders until 1911, when explorer Hiram Bingham, a U.S. senator turned archaeologist, stumbled across it while looking for another lost city. The origins and purpose of Machu Picchu, which means "ancient peak" in the local language, are still unknown, but some experts believe that the city may already have been abandoned before the Spanish conquest, which explains why it remained unknown to, and thus unvisited by, the Spanish. But it is clearly an Inca city, and because the Inca had only come to power a few decades before the conquest, this means that the city was built, used, and abandoned all within less than a century.

Recent theories suggest that it was a ceremonial site and perhaps an administrative center of a region with a substantial population, but that most people lived elsewhere in small villages. Whatever its purpose, it is today one of the most remarkable ancient ruins anywhere in the world. Dilwyn Jenkins, writing in *The Rough Guide to Peru*, comments that Machu Picchu is

> constructed on dizzying slopes overlooking a U-curve in the Rio Urubamba. More than a hundred flights of steep stone steps interconnect its palaces, temples, storehouses and terraces, and the outstanding views command not only the valley below in both directions but also extend to the snowy peaks around. Wherever you stand in the ruins, spectacular terraces can be seen slicing across ridiculously steep cliffs, transforming mountains into suspended gardens.

In late 2000 a company filming a beer advertisement accidentally knocked off a piece of one of the structures at the site, outraging people around the

world and calling into question the appropriateness of mixing the commercial and the historic in this manner.

Researchers theorize that Machu Picchu was a ceremonial site or possibly an administrative center.

and the Madeira, are formed from watershed from the high *selva*, and eventually feed into the Amazon, whose basin takes up nearly a quarter of the land mass of South America. Compared to the *selva* of the upper Amazon, the southern region is even more remote and unexplored, despite the fact that it has far more dry land and thus at least some roads. Even by road, however, the arduous three-hundred-mile-long trip from Cuzco to Puerto Maldonado takes three days.

Difficulty of access has enabled the region to benefit from efforts to protect its ecology. Of particular note is the Parque Nacional Manu, which covers a region larger than the country of Switzerland. Called a biosphere reserve, Manu's purpose is to teach both residents and visitors how to create an environment that supports human populations without destroying the region's ecology. Another important park is the Reserva Nacional Tambopata-Candamo. It is an "extractive reserve," which means that residents can continue to harvest products from the land, most notably Brazil nuts and rubber. However, they and the people who buy the products are being educated as to how to keep from destroying the local ecology and economy by overextraction. Ecotourism is also being encouraged, so that residents can recognize that such things as exotic birds and monkeys are of greater value to them live in the wild, rather than as products to be caught and sold. Whole villages can survive on money spent by tourists on lodging, food, and transportation, and with tourism carefully controlled to minimize environmental damage, the economic future of those who live in ecological reserves looks bright.

THE ANDES

One of the major mountain ranges of the world, the Andes run through the center of Peru. On the eastern flank of the Andes lies dense rain forest, but the lower reaches of the western Andes are as barren as the adjacent coastal desert. Between these two extremes lie many *cordilleras*, or ranges, all with their own names. The Andes rise quickly to great heights, and from almost any point along the coast, their snowcapped peaks are visible along the eastern horizon.

The Andes have two basic appearances. Along much of their length, they rise sharply to high, pointed peaks. The most dramatic and highest of this type of mountain are in the section known as the Cordillera Blanca. It is called *blanca*, or white, because it is perpetually covered in snow and is covered by huge glaciers in places. The Andes also have lower regions, primarily where the range widens in the southernmost parts of Peru. Land is still very mountainous in southern regions such as Puno and Arequipa, but peaks are lower and plateaus are more common.

Because of major variations in altitude and terrain, the Andes contain some of the harshest and most inaccessible landscapes in Peru, but also an astonishing number of small villages and cities, supporting over a third of Peru's total population. Andean populations tend to be densest in the regions where land can be cultivated. All in all, there is as much land under cultivation in the Andes as along the coast. Much of it consists of steeply terraced hillsides in regions where the elevation is not too high to preclude an adequate growing season or too rugged to permit

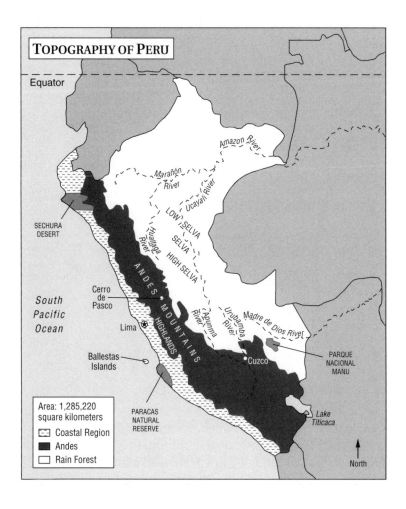

planting of typical Andean crops such as potatoes, yucca, and *quinoa*, a grain. Typically, the same valleys that are good for growing crops also have abundant pasturage for llamas, as well as vicuñas and alpacas, which are raised for their hair which is made into soft, high-quality yarn. Cows, goats, sheep, and other European livestock have also been successfully transplanted to the lower elevations in the Andes.

Residents of the Andes have been able to get around quite well for several millennia despite the terrain, where a mountain may fall almost vertically from 15,000 feet to a rushing river cut into a canyon of solid rock at about 3,000 feet in elevation, then almost immediately rise to 15,000 feet again. The Inca were masters at bridge building and created an advanced network of foot trails. Newer forms of travel such as railroads and highways were slow in arriving, and though the population centers are all reachable by many forms of transportation today, many of the more remote communities, especially in the higher stretches of the Andes, are still as isolated as their counterparts in the Amazon Basin.

Some parts of the Andes, most notably the region in the middle of the country known as Cerro del Pasco, are noted for their mineral wealth. Even at elevations as high as twelve thousand feet, prosperous communities can be found, and in some regions almost everyone depends on mining for their living. In other areas, mineral spas attract tourists. However, most tourists are drawn to the Andes not to visit spas but to experience the mountains' awesome beauty. Beautiful lakes such as Lake Titicaca, the highest navigable body of water in the world, along with volcanoes, dramatic terraced hillsides, steep peaks, and valleys make the Andes one of the most spectacular natural regions of the world.

Cuzco

Cuzco, the onetime center of the Inca Empire, is a vibrant city, one of the most important in Peru. It was the capital city of the Inca, so beautiful and advanced technologically that chroniclers traveling with Pizarro thought it more remarkable than anything in Spain. Cuzco remained important under the Spanish, serving as a cultural center for art and architecture. As a result, it has some of the finest colonial architecture in the world mixed in among the Inca ruins, which are still visible in town. Its cultural and architectural role has continued, most re-

A VOLATILE LANDSCAPE

Peru is located in a region of tremendous seismic activity known as the Cadena del Fuego, or Chain of Fire. The Andes were created eons ago by rock pushed up from deep underground as a result of this seismic activity, and movement under the earth's surface continues to cause frequent earthquakes today.

A major fault, or shifting crack in the earth, runs parallel to the Peruvian shoreline. It turns inland in the south, near Arequipa, and it is there that earthquakes create the most devastation. Though most villages consist of small adobe buildings that can withstand tremors or can be easily replaced, the biggest problem comes when the earthquakes dislodge huge amounts of rock and dirt from mountainsides in a phenomenon know to geologists as mass wasting. Sometimes the dislodged earth opens up chasms through which mountain lakes suddenly drain. Huge mudslides bury whole villages, entombing their inhabitants. The worst disaster of this sort occurred in 1970 in Yungay, near Huaraz, when the water of a lake suddenly came rushing downslope carrying soil and rocks with it, sweeping eighteen thousand people to their deaths. The mud has long since dried, but it is so deep it has erased all signs that the village ever existed, except for the tops of the three palm trees that once graced the village square and now protrude forlornly from the rocks and bare soil.

Earthquakes have played a major role in Peruvian history. One major earthquake destroyed much of the city of Lima in 1746. Another in Cuzco in 1650 is still commemorated today in the annual festival of Nuestro Señor de los Temblores, or

"Our Lord of the Earthquakes." A crucifix credited with miraculously saving the city is paraded around town on a beautiful silver platform, while people sprinkle flower petals in its path.

The spectacular Andes mountains, pictured here near Machu Picchu, resulted from tremendous seismic activity.

cently through a new building campaign in the 1990s, which produced modern fountains and statues based on Inca designs. Because the Inca considered Cuzco the navel of the universe, it is a magnet for visitors with mystical leanings. It is also

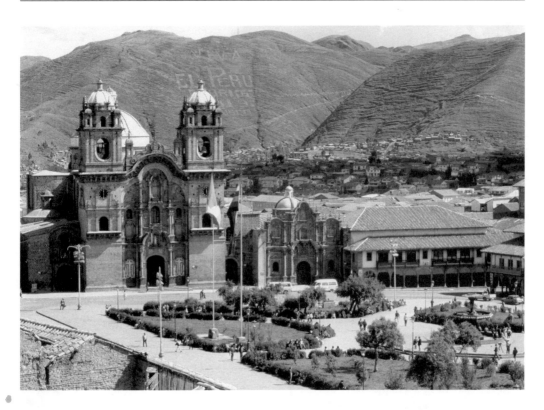

The architecture of buildings such as La Compania Cathedral on the Plaza de las Armas helps draw tourists to Cuzco.

the jumping-off point for trips to Manu, the Nazca plain, Machu Picchu, and many other Inca and pre-Inca sites.

Cuzco is, according to Jenkins, "one of South America's biggest tourist destinations."[10] Perhaps this is because in many ways it captures in one place all that is most special about Peru, which is itself one of the most unusual and interesting places on earth.

The Inca and Intruders

For centuries Spanish and other explorers headed to South America to search for El Dorado, the fabled city of gold. For many, the ultimately futile search for this nonexistent city began in Peru, for it was thought that if any South American culture was capable of creating a city where gems were playthings and everyday objects were made of gold, it would have arisen there. In Peru, advanced civilizations had already flourished for several millennia. In fact, the famous civilization of the Inca was only about a century old at the time of the arrival of the Spanish in 1532, having been established after conquering and assimilating several earlier advanced civilizations along the western coast of South America.

The Spaniards may have been wrong about the existence of El Dorado, but they nevertheless managed to become rich beyond their wildest dreams by exploiting the resources of the region and subjecting the Peruvian people to conditions of near slavery. It took less than forty years from the time of the arrival of the Spanish for Tupac Amarú, the last Inca leader, to fall and for the people of the region to decline into poverty and backwardness. For 250 years, Peru was ruled by the Spanish, whose exploitation, arrogance, and cruelty destroyed much of the indigenous culture and laid the foundation for the troubled modern nation of Peru. By the time Peru declared independence in 1821, it had become an uneasy mix of native and colonial culture, a country proudly invoking its history as evidence of its ability to govern itself, but battered by centuries of subjugation. Anxious to assert its identity as an independent nation, Peru was not sure any more what its true identity really was.

The Initial Period

Early Peruvians had no such questions about their culture. Human civilization in Peru goes back well over four thousand years, and according to Adriana van Hagen, writing in *Insight*

Guide: Peru, "The earliest monumental architecture is roughly contemporary with the pyramids of Egypt."[11] Human civilization existed in the region as far back as 12,000 B.C., and by approximately 2500 B.C. small but sophisticated villages dotted the coast. In these villages early Peruvians not only fished and hunted deer and other game, but also planted cotton, creating threads that they entwined and looped into textiles long before the invention of the loom for weaving. Archaeological evidence of the existence of these early people has been unearthed north of Lima.

Around 1800 B.C., in the era known to anthropologists as the Initial Period, the coastal people began moving inland. Although they remained within a dozen or so miles of the coast, they were able to increase the amount of land available for agriculture by using river water channeled through irrigation ditches. The diet of the people of the Initial Period was well balanced and food was plentiful, consisting of squashes, peppers, various beans, avocados, and other food crops, in addition to fish and game. Though life was hard, the development of agriculture meant that early Peruvians did not have to spend all their time searching for food. It is in this era that the first decorative pottery and woven cloth was produced, art forms that would evolve into hallmarks of Peruvian culture throughout the centuries.

Also in this era, people began to build monuments, most of which have been unearthed only in the last century. At Moxeke, in the Casma Valley north of Lima, a ninety-foot-high painted adobe pyramid covered with raised designs called friezes was excavated and restored. Farther up the coast, other adobe structures, as well as platforms and sunken courtyards, have been found, decorated with faded designs depicting wild animals and humans. The best-known site from the Initial Period is Sechin, which consists of an adobe pyramid surrounded by stone pillars on which are carved battle scenes, including a scene of a victorious army bringing back the dismembered corpses of their enemy.

THE CHAVÍN, NAZCA, AND MOCHE CULTURES

Farther inland, in the foothills and highlands at the base of the Andes, other cultures were also evolving. Around 800 B.C. the most advanced early culture, the Chavín, rose in the region around Huaraz. Its influence spread as far as the Bay of Paracas, about a hundred miles south of Lima, where recently un-

This depiction of a warrior was one of many carvings found at the ruins in Sechin.

earthed mummies have been found wrapped in painted cotton textiles that are, according to van Hagen, "perhaps the finest cloth ever produced in ancient Peru, [using] almost every technique known to [today's] Andean weaver."[12] Some of their cottons were so fine, they resembled silk and were "dyed in at least 109 hues in 7 natural color categories."[13] The Chavín culture established extensive trade networks, as evidenced by items found in burial mounds, including tropical feathers presumed to have come from the Amazon Basin on the other side of the Andes. The oldest known gold and silver objects also date from this era.

Other cultures dominated different parts of Peru in the era from approximately 300 B.C. to A.D. 600, known to archaeologists as the Early Intermediate Period. Perhaps the best known of these is the Nazca, who inhabited a dry plain north of the modern city of the same name. On this plain the Nazca people etched huge designs, by carving and sweeping away soil and rocks until lighter-colored soil at deeper levels emerged. The oldest images, some as big as two hundred feet in diameter, are of animals such as birds, killer whales, spiders, and monkeys. The carvings continued to be made over several hundred years, but later ones tended to be geometric designs rather than recognizable animal figures.

According to archaeologist Brian Fagan, power at this time began to be measured by the "ability to marshal large numbers of people for impressive public works in the name of the gods."[14] One powerful group by this standard was the Moche, who lived in the Trujillo, or Moche Valley, in the northern coastal region of today's Peru. Archaeological evidence suggests that they were the most advanced of the cultures of the Early Intermediate Period. In addition to constructing monuments and grand buildings, they developed systems of irrigation that stretched for many miles, even bringing water from one valley to another. The Moche domesticated dogs and other animals and made beautiful jewelry set with precious stones from faraway places, evidence of their extensive trade networks. They were excellent ceramicists and potters and, according to van Hagen, also "perfected an electrochemical plating system that gilded copper objects."[15]

OTHER PRE-INCA CULTURES

Two other cultures helped shape Peru in the period before the Inca. The first of these, the Wari, rose in the Ayacucho region not far from Nazca, around A.D. 800. Evidence is scanty as to why the Nazca and other groups of the Early Intermediate Period were overtaken by the Wari, but it is clear that, for whatever reason, the Wari were dominant over much of the highlands and coast of Peru. Military outposts have been discovered as far north as Trujillo, as far east as Cuzco, and as far south as Lake Titicaca. The Wari have been linked to a site in Tihaunaco in today's Bolivia, where an ingenious system of planting involved dredging swampy land around a lake to create artificial islands on which potatoes and grains were grown.

THE NAZCA LINES

On the barren plains of Nazca lies one of the great archaeological mysteries of the ancient world. There, long, wide lines were cut into the ground until a contrasting color of rock or soil was reached. These lines are not random, but in fact form beautiful geometric shapes, animal figures, and other designs similar to those found on the pottery of the ancient Nazca people, who lived long before the Inca Empire. The designs, carved around A.D. 600, are very large, up to 1,000 feet in diameter. They include a monkey 300 feet across, a spider 150 feet long, and a bird 200 feet across. There is no way for the shapes to be seen from the ground, and there are no nearby mountain vantage points. The designs, therefore, can only be appreciated from the air, even though they were created many centuries before the first known human flight.

The meaning and purpose of these lines can only be guessed at, for the answers died out with the Nazca people themselves. In the 1970s Erich von Daniken proposed that the lines had been created by visitors from outer space, although archaeologists are doubtful of this idea. The theories of Maria Reiche, a mathematician who devoted her life to studying the Nazca Lines, are the most widely supported today. She argued, based on astronomical evidence and the documented interest of the Nazca people in the stars, that the drawings are both an astronomical calendar and a way of sending messages to the gods. For example, the constellation we know as the Big Dipper looked like a monkey to the Nazca. According to author Pam Barrett, in Reiche's theory, "when rain was overdue—a common thing in this plain—the Nazca people sketched the monkey to remind the gods that the earth was parched."

But the question of how the Nazca got the perspective to create such symmetrical patterns is as yet unanswered, though the International Explorers Club set out in 1975 to show that it would have been possible for the Nazca people to have

created hot air balloons using only cloth and reeds. The experimental flight lasted one minute and reached an altitude of three hundred feet, hardly convincing evidence, but adding yet one more idea to the many that surround this ancient mystery.

The Nazca Lines form huge designs, such as this 300-foot monkey, which can only be appreciated from the air.

UNCOVERING THE PAST

Two of the best-known sites of pre-Inca Peru have been found at the similarly named towns of Sipán and Sican, both in the northern part of the country. Originally uncovered by looters looking for treasure, the grave site at Sipán yielded a skeleton now called, for want of a more precise name, the Lord of Sipán. Believed to have been a Moche ruler sometime between A.D. 100 and 700, he was buried with an astonishing collection of gold and copper masks and headdresses, turquoise and lapis lazuli jewelry, as well as fine examples of Moche pottery and ceramics. Vital information about the Moche culture has come from this site.

At Sican archaeologists used radar for the first time to locate the prime underground sites. They found riches similar to those at Moche, but from another culture that arose later, around the ninth century. All over Peru similar sites continue to be found, but unfortunately many of them are located first by looters and grave robbers, who seek to make fortunes from the relics. According to Pam Barrett, writing in *Insight Guide: Peru*, "Priceless treasures have been lifted from graves all over Peru and sold to collectors. Around the Cemetery of Chauchilla, near Nazca, the desert is strewn with bones and skulls unearthed by *huaqueros* (robbers), stripped of valuables, and left to bleach in the sun." Rewards for turning in traffickers in looted treasure are now offered, but the best answer seems to be to find and protect the sites first. Aerial surveillance to look for evidence of new sites is also used to catch looters in the act.

The overnight frosts that would otherwise have killed these crops were kept at bay by the radiated warmth of the water, which collected heat from the sun during the day. Recent attempts to grow crops in this manner indicate that yields could have been as much as seven times greater than for the same crops grown by other methods in the area.

The Wari were militarily stronger than any other group before them, but they were less inclined than other early Peruvian groups had been to adopt practices and traditions of the people they came to dominate. The Wari were therefore responsible for destroying much of the culture and archaeological record of those who had preceded them. However, with the eventual decline of the Wari, many other regional cultures began to thrive once again. The most notable of these is the Sican, in the north around Chiclayo, about whom little is known except that their rulers' graves contain a wide range of high-quality gold and silver pieces, often encrusted with gems, which suggests both a wealthy and powerful culture and a center of metallurgy.

Later, around A.D. 1000, two other groups, the Chachapoya and the Chimu, emerged as the dominant powers in their regions, the northern highlands and the northern coast, respectively. Next to nothing is known about the Chachapoya, but Chimu legends were passed down orally until the arrival of the Spanish, at which time these stories were written down. Therefore, more particulars of the Chimu culture are known than those of previous groups, such as the names of many of their rulers. The Chimu also left behind a remarkable capital city, Chan Chan, the largest adobe city in the world. Chan Chan was the center of their far-flung empire (the largest to date in Peru) until it fell to the Inca in 1464.

At its height, approximately fifty thousand people lived in Chan Chan, and the city stretched over nine square miles— huge by ancient standards. In Chimu culture, rule was not passed down through a family line from father to son, so there was no permanent royal family. The ruler was very powerful while alive, building a compound that housed his own court, family home, administrative buildings, and storehouses. Upon his death he was entombed in his compound, and his entourage remained there for the rest of their lives tending the ruler's mummified remains and otherwise showing their continued loyalty, but having no further political power. The new ruler built his own compound, following the same basic pattern. Altogether ten compounds survive, most in a ruined state, representing ten monarchs.

THE RISE OF THE INCA

Each dominant group had to this point controlled a larger territory than the one before it, but expansion carried with it problems. Lacking both horses and the technology of the wheel, people traveled mostly on foot, often over treacherous terrain. Communication with outlying regions of the empire was difficult, and additional troops could not easily be brought in to help local units quell revolts. Therefore, wide-ranging power was hard to hold on to. Though archaeological evidence demonstrates that groups such as the Chimu had armies stationed in strategic places over a wide territory, their control of that territory was shaky at best.

The Inca began as one of many small groups in the central highlands. By 1400, during the reign of Pachacutec, they were poised for the meteoric rise that would make them one of the great powers of the western hemisphere within a period of only fifty years. At its peak the Inca Empire was as large as the ancient Roman Empire, extending far beyond the boundaries of today's Peru, north into Colombia and south into Chile.

The Inca had several characteristics that distinguished them from the Chimu and most other groups before them. First, they were intensely interested in and respectful of the achievements of other regional cultures. Historian Peter Frost explains, "As each regional culture fell, Inca teachers, weavers, builders and metallurgists studied the conquered people's textile techniques, architecture, gold-working, irrigation, pottery and healing methods. As a result, they quickly accumulated massive amounts of information more advanced than their own."[16]

The Inca were also more politically astute than any other group before them. They recognized that they would not be able to keep control of their rapidly expanding empire by force, and thus they allowed neighboring cultures to retain much of their autonomy as long as they swore loyalty to the Inca leadership and worshiped the Inca gods. Those who resisted, however, were dealt with harshly. Many were removed from their ancestral lands and forcibly resettled where population growth was needed and where they would be easier to keep an eye on. Their chiefs were brought to Cuzco, the Inca capital, and kept as "guests" under house arrest for the rest of their lives.

THE PEAK OF INCA POWER

The Inca called their empire Tahuantinsuya, meaning the Kingdom of the Four Quarters. With Cuzco at its center, the empire was divided into four regions and stretched for twenty-five hundred miles along the coast and east into the Andes. Communication was remarkably good as a result of a system of narrow footpaths that crisscrossed the empire, dotted approximately every six miles by a lodge called a *tambo* where food and goods in transit were stored and traveling groups of people were sheltered. Every hut had a resident *quipucamayoc* who made a record of everything of value or interest that passed through the *tambo*, using an elaborate system of knotted string called a *quipu*. Even closer together were the *chasquis*, huts where runners stayed. These runners conveyed messages, sprinting the two-mile distance between huts at such a high speed that messages may have traveled as much as fifteen hundred miles, the distance between Cuzco and Quito (now in Ecuador but then the capital of the northern Inca Empire) in five days.

The Inca proved to be adept at developing and managing their empire. Using a communal workforce known as the *mita*, they demanded of each village a contribution of labor to help build and maintain the empire. One village might be required to send young men as soldiers, while another might be required to grow grain for storage, and another might supply workers for the building of a palace or ceremonial site or for work in mines. The Inca constantly strove to improve communication across their empire by building roads. Villages near the long woven suspension bridges that connected roads across deep river canyons fulfilled their *mita* obligation by keeping the bridge in working order, and villages at the river's edge usually fulfilled theirs by building and maintaining pontoon bridges.

By using the workforce at their disposal, the Inca were able to develop great stores of food, communication networks, and other necessary resources that they used to create loyalty and dependence. According to Frost, "Inca society was clearly hierarchical and highly structured, but not necessarily tyrannical or repressive. Life wasn't easy, but food and resources were stored and distributed so that all were fed and clothed."[17] Though not all Peruvians of this era accepted Inca domination willingly, it is likely that most, especially those close to the center of Inca power, felt loyalty to the Inca leaders who had brought such progress and prosperity to the region. *Mita* service also allowed many people to travel far away from home and see some of the fabulous sights of the Inca Empire, and this also contributed to a sense of pride and loyalty.

Frost explains, "The glue holding the empire together was the practice of reciprocity: ritual

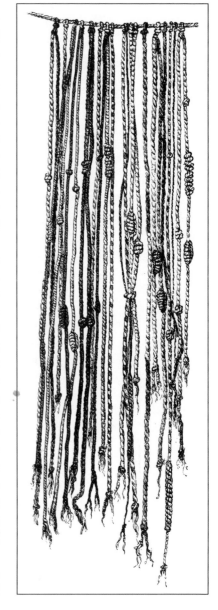

The Inca kept records using a quipu, *a system of knotted strings.*

generosity and favors to local rulers on a huge scale in exchange for loyalty, labor and military levies, women for the
Inca nobility . . . and so on. The emperor maintained fabulous
stores of goods to meet his ritual obligations and create new alliances."[18] Thus the greatest empire in precolonial Latin America was built almost overnight. But it was not without its
problems and political struggles. As the Inca moved farther
afield in the "four quarters," they came across groups who were
more difficult to subjugate because they had less in common
culturally and historically with people of the Peruvian highlands, from which the Inca had come. The Inca were not particularly warlike; despite their stunning accomplishments in
other endeavors, their only weapons were primitive clubs,
wooden spears, and stones. They often relied simply on the
size of their army to terrorize foes and generally preferred
diplomacy and alliances as a means of empire building. They
continued to expand their empire, but it was getting more difficult to control.

Several developments soon set in motion the eventual
decline of the empire. First, a group of coastal Peruvians
known as the Chanca, who believed based on their mythol-
ogy that they were the legitimate rulers of the region, attacked Cuzco. Huayna Capac, the current Inca—as the ruler
was known (the term "Inca" did not apply to all the people
of the empire until later)—retreated to Quito with his son
and heir, Atahualpa, installing another younger son, Huáscar, as ruler of the Cuzco-centered part of the empire. Huáscar proved to be quite a hero, fending off the Chanca attack
and creating a strong core of powerful supporters among
the nobility and priests. Quarrels between the two brothers
eventually arose as to who was the legitimate Inca, or ruler,
of the whole empire, and this enmity undermined the Inca
Empire. When Huayna Capac died of smallpox, which had
swept south from Mexico after being brought to the New
World by the Spaniards, Huáscar and Atahualpa engaged in
several bloody battles, with Atahualpa emerging as the vic-
tor. The last of these took place in 1532, and it was while
Atahualpa was recovering with his troops at some nearby
thermal baths that he got word that pale-skinned, bearded
men had landed with sailing ships on the north Peruvian
coast.

THE SPANISH CONQUEST

The leader of these new arrivals was Francisco Pizarro. His entire party consisted of only 170 soldiers and a few miscellaneous travelers, including a priest, Vicente de Valverde. From their landing point at Tumbes, they followed the coast south until they were met by an envoy of Atahualpa, who invited them to meet the Inca at the city of Cajamarca, deep in the Andes. Pizarro was so confident of his men's ability to overcome the forty thousand or more Inca soldiers encamped nearby that he and Valverde marched into the square where the meeting was to take place. Valverde handed Atahualpa a Bible, telling him he was there to save his soul. When an unimpressed Atahualpa let the book fall to the ground, Pizarro treated this as an offense against God and ordered his well-armed soldiers to attack. Despite their superior numbers, the Inca were defeated and Atahualpa was captured. Atahualpa offered to ransom himself by filling several rooms with gold and silver brought from all over his empire, and although Pizarro took the treasure, totaling twenty-four tons, he did not free Atahualpa. Rather, he gave him the choice of dying as a heathen by burning at the stake or as a baptized Christian by strangulation with a garrote. Atahualpa chose the latter and was executed in August 1533.

Inca ruler Atahualpa, Spanish priest Vicente de Valverde, and Spanish explorer Francisco Pizarro meet in Cajamarca, Peru.

Author Holligan de Diaz-Limaco writes, "It was the very nature of the Inca Empire and the civil war [between Atahualpa and Huáscar] that allowed Pizarro to build on this audacious start and take over Cuzco."[19] Pizarro knew that support for Atahualpa was weak in Cuzco, which had been Huáscar's base, and that he was likely to be greeted as a hero there for toppling Atahualpa. He also knew that many parts of the empire resented Inca rule altogether and would show no real loyalty in a showdown between the Inca and the Spanish. Pizarro was able to take advantage of the Inca system of roads, *mita*, and other innovations to take quick control of the empire. What Pizarro could not take over in this fashion, he got by brute force in a series of battles and terrorist campaigns in all four quarters.

Greed eventually was the undoing of Pizarro, who was murdered by followers of Diego de Almagro, a former partner of Pizarro's in the conquest of Peru. Almagro had been murdered by Pizarro in a 1538 dispute over how to split control of the empire between them, and Pizarro's murder was payback for that. Vicente de Valverde, the priest who had handed the Bible to Atahualpa and thus set in motion the first attack on the Inca people by the Spaniards, also came to a grisly end, probably eaten by cannibals after the wreck of the ship on which he had attempted to escape after Pizarro's murder.

But the story of the Inca was not quite over. A grandson of Atahualpa, Titi Cusi, was named Inca by a group of followers living in exile in the Amazon. He died suddenly of unknown reasons after drinking a potion several missionaries had given him to remedy an illness, and when the missionaries were bru-

MANCO INCA

The Inca did not give up their empire to the Spanish *conquistadores* without resistance. Manco Inca, one of Huayna Capac's sons, was a puppet ruler who did the bidding of the Spanish for a while after Atahualpa's death. Soon he came to see the brutality and lack of principles of the Spanish, who wasted no time before they began extorting gold and other treasure, pillaging property, enslaving indigenous people, and raping Inca women, including Manco's wife. In 1536 Manco secretly mobilized loyal chiefs and soldiers and escaped into the Andes to plan a rebellion. Much of the Inca capital of Cuzco was eventually recaptured by Manco's army, but the Spanish counterattacked with fresh troops. Manco was eventually forced into the jungle, where he ran a government in exile for thirty-five years until his death.

After conquering the Inca and taking twenty-four tons of treasure, Pizarro ordered the execution of Atahualpa.

tally killed in revenge, the Spanish had all the motive they needed to move in to finish off the last shreds of the Inca Empire. By then a new leader, Tupac Amarú, had emerged after Titi Cusi's death. Though he put up remarkably strong resistance against the Spanish, he was eventually captured, tried, and beheaded in 1572 for the murder of the Spanish priests. After his death the remaining Inca put up no more resistance, and one of the world's great cultures unceremoniously came to an end. The Spaniards had what they wanted—an El Dorado of a different sort, one where riches might not lie strewn on the ground like pebbles, but could be obtained easily enough by exploiting the once-mighty Inca. It would be several centuries before the people of Peru once again had a chance to take control of their own lives and rule in their own country.

3

FROM COLONY TO CONTEMPORARY NATION

In the nearly two centuries following the Spanish invasion, Peruvians had little chance of coexisting well with their conquerors. Besides being no match for the Spaniards militarily, they also died in huge numbers as a result of lack of immunity to European diseases. Smallpox, measles, and even the common cold reduced an indigenous population of approximately 9 million at the time of the conquest by more than half in a few decades, and to 600,000 in a century. Eventually, when Spain declined as a world power in the late eighteenth and early nineteenth century, Peru declared independence, but the long period of Spanish rule had created many social problems whose legacy continues into the present.

THE *ENCOMIENDAS*

The Spanish initially were satisfied by looting Inca treasures from Cuzco and other sites, keeping some items for themselves and sending shiploads of precious gold and silver objects back as tribute to the Spanish monarch. Eventually, however, the supply of things to pillage began to run out, and a new base for the colonial economy was needed. The *encomienda* system was introduced, whereby Spanish nobles and others were given tracts of land by the Spanish monarch as payment for services rendered or as a sign of royal favor. The monarch retained land title and in theory could take the land back if an *encomendero*, or landholder, displeased him or her. All *encomenderos* were expected to pay heavy tribute to the monarch from the profits of their land as a sign of their gratitude and loyalty.

The gift of an *encomienda* included not only the land itself but the right to the labor of the people who lived on it. Thus, many Peruvians who had lived in freedom suddenly found themselves subject to someone who had been given rights to their ancestral lands. They could not leave, for they were considered permanently bound to the land they lived on and part of its overall value. They were technically not slaves because they belonged to the land, not directly to a person, but practically speaking there is very little difference between this state, called serfdom, and slavery.

Indeed, the *encomenderos* treated the indigenous Peruvians like slaves. The labor of some as soldiers and workers on government building projects was offered by *encomenderos* as part of their tribute, and many Peruvians would find themselves summarily marched off from their villages to serve as laborers,

THE PERUVIAN CATHOLIC CHURCH

Not all people came to Peru to find wealth. Catholic priests generally accompanied voyages of discovery to begin what Spaniards felt to be the essential task of converting everyone in the world to Christianity. This proved difficult in Peru. According to Adriana van Hagen, writing in *Insight Guide: Peru*, "In many ways the Catholic campaign served to entrench native beliefs; rather than taking over, Christianity formed a thin veneer over traditional cults and beliefs, many of which still exist today." Priests who could not persuade villagers to abandon traditional ways often resorted to torture and wholesale destruction of religious objects. However, their journals and other works (such as the more than one thousand drawings and maps with accompanying notes by an eighteenth-century bishop, Martinez de Compagnon) provide much of the information available today about the colonial era in rural Peru.

The priest's role quickly expanded as rivalries grew between powerful *encomenderos* and new royal authorities called *corregimentos*, who served as governors of local areas. Arguments over duties owed by *encomenderos* to the king and attempts to curb their growing power often had to be mediated by priests. Later in the colonial period, after the fervor to convert Peruvians had abated, most clerics stayed in cities and towns. There they took on the traditional role of parish priest, serving local populations of Spaniards and people of mixed blood, who frequently embraced Christianity as a means of social progress. Over time the Catholic Church collected such extensive holdings of land and wealth that it was the most powerful economic force in Peru, richer by far than any *encomendero*. It was the main educator and provider of social services, and, according to Rex A. Hudson, writing for the Library of Congress in *Peru: A Country Study*, its close relationship of mutual support with the Spanish Crown, "despite awesome problems of distance, rough terrain, and slow communications, endured almost three centuries of continuous and relatively stable rule."

usually never to return. Though remaining in the Spanish monarch's favor was important to the *encomenderos*, they also exploited Indian labor to build their personal fortunes. Spanish colonists forced villagers to work the fields for long hours every day. If the people of a particular village could be put to better use, or perhaps better controlled elsewhere, their whole village would be relocated with no regard for their ties to the land. These forced relocations into *reducciónes*, new villages, were devastating to indigenous communities.

Encomenderos also found ways to put to economic use those Peruvians who lived on land that could not easily be farmed or ranched. In the seventeenth century, many of the healthiest and strongest Peruvian youth were marched high into the Andes to the silver mines at Potosí, now in Bolivia, and to the mercury mines in nearby Huancavelica. There, they were forced to work under conditions that very often killed them outright or at least considerably shortened their lives due to accidents, poisonous gases, malnutrition, and overwork. According to author Jenkins, "Few Indians who left to work in the mines ever returned. Those who were taken to Potosí had to be chained together to stop them from escaping."[20] Though the Spanish invoked the Inca tradition of *mita* as a grounds for demanding Indian labor, unlike the *mita*, the profits from the mines were not channeled back as a community resource. Local communities lost the people they most needed to sustain themselves and ensure future generations, and they received nothing in compensation. Over time these greedy tactics by the Spanish further undermined Peruvian life.

THE RISE OF *CRIOLLO* CULTURE

As the silver mines began to produce less and less in the eighteenth century, and as exports in general decreased, the Crown's profit from the colony dwindled. Peru, however, continued to prosper internally. Its diversity of crops and products made it easily able to support itself and create a healthy economy by regional trade, without reliance on Europe. A new influx of Spanish immigrants seeking a better life in the New World had taken over coastal agricultural land, much of which had lain vacant since its former residents were killed off by smallpox or other causes. Like many colonists elsewhere, the new arrivals were not from wealthy or noble families, but were ordinary people seeking to rise economically and socially through their own efforts. Many of them worked very hard to develop agriculture not just along

THE *CRIOLLOS*

The *criollos* formed a new middle class in a society highly sensitive to ethnicity and national origin. Over fifty terms were commonly in use in colonial Peru for all possible ethnic mixes, including many such as *mestizo* and *mulatto* that survive today; but there was no doubt that European-born people were at the top of society and the darkest-skinned people were at the bottom. Some *criollos*, largely due to their European appearance, eventually were accepted into the elite of society, especially after the mid-1600s, when the Spanish monarch began selling royal appointments and offices to the highest bidders. *Criollos* could thus buy the prestige they craved, but according to Library of Congress researcher Rex A. Hudson, in *Peru: A Country Study*, "Lamentably the sale of public offices also had longer-term implications." The nobility saw an element of social obligation in their privileged status: They were expected to show at least some concern for the less fortunate at least from time to time and not appear too greedy or ambitious. If they held any public or political office, it was seen as a duty, not an achievement. Selling public offices, according to Hudson, "weakened any notion of disinterested public service and [introduced] the corrosive idea that public office-holding was an opportunity for selfish, private gain, rather than for the general public good." That attitude became an important—and damaging—factor in politics even into contemporary times.

the coast but also in the central valleys and highlands. Grapes, olives, sugar, and other new crops flourished in these locales.

The offspring of these Spanish immigrants were usually referred to as *criollos*, or Creoles, an imprecise term for people of European blood born in the New World. While the vast majority of Peruvians were trying simply to survive their oppression by adapting where they could and avoiding contact with Europeans of all sorts whenever possible, *criollos* became more and more important politically, socially, and economically. Peru, largely due to the efforts of *criollos*, was rapidly becoming a prosperous center of trade, as evidenced by the growth of its new capital city, Lima.

The Inca had not been a seafaring people, and thus their cities tended to rise up away from the coast, often in rather inaccessible places that would be easier to defend against outsiders. The Spanish, however, relied on the seas for transportation and trade, and from the beginning of the colonial period, trade centers sprang up all along the Central and South American coast. Francisco Pizarro founded Lima in 1535, shortly after his conquest of the Inca, and it quickly became the capital of Spanish South America, which by then also included Ecuador, Bolivia, and Chile. Known as the City of Kings, Lima had an enviable location, situated in a large river valley, with a good natural harbor nearby and relatively easy access into the Andes. The importance of Lima was enhanced by the decision of the Spanish monarchy to require that all export and import trade go through the customhouses there. Jenkins writes that Lima "remained the most important, the richest and . . . the most alluring city in South America until the early nineteenth century."[21] It housed the first university in South America, the University of San Marcos, founded in 1551, as well as many mansions and government buildings looking out onto beautiful tree-lined streets and plazas. It also was home to a thriving marketplace, and within a few decades of its founding, "the center of Lima was crowded with shops and stalls selling silks and fancy furniture from as far afield as China."[22]

The faces of the residents of Lima reflected just how much and how quickly the region had changed since the conquest. The 1610 census revealed that blacks (mostly brought as slaves) comprised 40 percent of the population. Spaniards made up 38 percent, and another 8 percent were of unspecified origin. The rest were indigenous Peruvians, only about 8 percent of whom were of pure Indian blood. Built essentially from scratch rather than evolving from a previous city inhabited by native people, Lima, unlike Cuzco and other older cities, grew without the reference point of native culture, and thus little blending of cultures occurred in the most politically and economically powerful city of western South America. Residents of Lima lived in a different world from the rest of Peru, a fact that has consequences even today.

REBELLIONS AND REVOLUTIONS

Most of the colonial period passed without historical incidents of great note. However, by the late 1700s a fervor for independence grew across South America, fanned first by the American Revolution and then by the revolution in France. Rebel leaders became common in the eighteenth century. Juan Santos Atahualpa—a *mestizo* (person of mixed Indian and Spanish blood) from Cuzco who traveled to Europe in service of a Jesuit

TUPAC AMARÚ II: THE LAST INCA

The Inca Empire fell quickly to the Spanish *conquistadores,* but despite the hopelessness of rebellion, even a century later some Inca were not willing to accept their defeat. In 1780 a descendant of Inca nobility, José Gabriel Condorcanqui, renamed himself Tupac Amarú II and began a rebellion against the Spanish. The indigenous people of Peru believed that the spirit of their ancient rulers would return to lead them back to their former glory, and Condorcanqui hoped they would believe he was indeed that reincarnated spirit. Many believed fervently in him, and others followed him because he promised relief from the oppression of the Spanish. After a few dramatic and violent acts against the Spanish, Tupac Amarú II was forced to retreat deep into the *selva* with his family and followers, including his pregnant wife. When he stopped to wait for his wife to give birth, Spanish soldiers caught up with him and took him to prison.

After a short trial he was sentenced to death. Rather than execute him quickly and as painlessly as possible, the Spanish forced him to watch while his wife and children were murdered. Then he was drawn and quartered, a gruesome death

caused by tying one's arms and legs to four horses and sending them running in different directions. The various portions of his body were displayed in the towns where his support had been the strongest. The Spanish viceroy at the same time declared that wearing Inca ceremonial clothing or participating in any traditional activities would be punished by death.

After Condorcanqui's death no one else ever declared himself the new Inca, but there is still a belief among some peasants today that one will emerge someday to liberate them from poverty and oppression and restore their culture to glory.

A Peruvian holds a portrait of Tupac Amarú II, a descendant of the Inca who proclaimed himself a reincarnated spirit of the ancient Inca rulers.

priest and was exposed to revolutionary ideas there—established a jungle community in the 1740s, expelling all whites from the area and living there with his followers for the rest of his life. But the most famous rebel was Tupac Amarú II, whose army massacred many colonial soldiers in the Cuzco area and embarrassed the colonial administration in the early 1780s before Amarú's grisly death at Spanish hands.

By this time newspapers advocating the end of monarchical rule in Peru had become common in the cities. They were supported by the growing *criollo* middle class, who stood to benefit the most if the nobility were no longer backed by the Spanish Crown. Rid of the nobility, they reasoned, the elite of Peru would consist of those like themselves, who had built their own fortunes rather than inheriting social standing by an accident of birth.

By the end of the eighteenth century, *criollos* had lived for so many generations in Peru that they thought of themselves as Peruvians, and a new sense of Peruvian nationalism, no longer Indian in origin but built around European ideas and culture, began to emerge. This nationalism was helped by political conditions in Europe. The French emperor Napoléon took control of Spain in 1808, removing the king from the throne and installing his own brother as monarch. In Peru, and throughout Central and South America, it was suddenly unclear to whom colonial allegiance lay. Revolutions around the world and this uncertainty at home pointed Peruvians in the direction of declaring independence themselves.

When the Spanish monarchy was restored in 1814 after the fall of Napoléon, it was too weak to defend its colonies. Venezuela and Argentina had already declared independence, and Chile followed in 1817. Peru still had many strong and powerful supporters of continued colonial rule, however, because of Lima's favored status as a port. As a result, the newly independent nations around it were concerned that if Peru remained a Spanish colony, it could serve as a base for Spain to invade and retake its former colonies. Revolutionary leaders Simon Bolívar from the north and José de San Martín from the south both independently moved toward Peru to lead a revolution there. San Martín, who had led the successful Chilean bid for independence, arrived first. After establishing a clear base of support in coastal towns, he attacked Lima. Those loyal to Spain fled for the hills, and on July 28, 1821, San Martín declared Peru an independent nation.

THE NEW REPUBLIC OF PERU

Independent status proved far easier to achieve than to maintain. Peru was not prepared to handle all the details and problems of self-rule. Peru quickly elected a parliament and turned to Simon Bolívar, the famous leader of the Venezuelan revolution, to be its first ruler. Bolívar agreed to the idea as part of his grand scheme for a regional superpower, "Gran Colombia," comprising Venezuela, Colombia, Ecuador, and Peru. Bolívar led Peru only for a little over two years (1824–27) until the last Spanish loyalists had been defeated in scattered fighting, before returning to deal with the demands of the nations to the north that he had led to independence.

After Bolívar's departure, an era of tremendous chaos ensued. Leaders such as José de la Mar, who replaced Bolívar, made sweeping promises to indigenous peoples that they made little effort to keep. Battles in many areas had wiped out food supplies, and many rural Peruvians, mostly Indians, found themselves in worse shape than at any time in memory. In the cities political differences and power struggles created chaos, and Peru had thirty-five changes of government between 1827 and 1865 alone. Most of these changes were the result of military leaders using

Revolutionary leader Simon Bolívar became Peru's first ruler in 1824.

their troops to overthrow one government in favor of their own inevitably short-lived ones.

Despite the chaos among the military elite who strove for political control of the country, "what is perhaps most extraordinary about Peru's independence," argues Holligan de Diaz-Limaco, "is how little changed in its wake."[23] Those who had enjoyed privileges under the Spanish created a world in which the same privileges continued to fall to them, and Peruvian society continued to remain as divided between poor and well-to-do as ever. Government exercised very little real control over life in Peru, and the country was nearly bankrupt despite the immense wealth of some of its citizens.

Things worsened in 1879 when Chile declared war against Bolivia and Peru over Tarapacá, a border region controlled by Peru that was rich in nitrates and borax, valuable minerals on the world market. Chilean military strength was so far superior to Peru's that Chile actually occupied Lima for a while and cut it off from contact with the rest of Peru. Known as the War of the Pacific, this conflict lasted for four years, ending in a treaty signed in 1883 that ceded Tarapacá to Chile.

The extent of the resulting damage to the Peruvian economy was offset briefly by several economic boosts, including a rubber boom in the Amazon that lasted approximately three decades between 1880 to 1910. A process called "vulcanization" invented by Charles Goodyear transformed the soft latex tapped from rubber trees into a product that would stay hard at high temperatures and thus could be used to make tires and other items useful to industry. Because rubber trees grew naturally nowhere else in the world, they were a source of enormous wealth. But when rubber trees planted experimentally elsewhere in the world reached maturity, competition resulted in a drastic reduction in the price of latex on world markets.

NEW PARTIES EMERGE

For several decades after the rubber boom ended, Peru was in such deep economic trouble that it had to agree to whatever conditions foreign nations and corporations imposed upon it to settle its debts. U.S. investors, for example, soon controlled mining in central Peru, enforcing working conditions as bad as those during colonial days and funneling profits out of the country rather than using them in a way that benefited Peru-

GUANO

The islands off Peru's coast make excellent sanctuaries for birds, and where birds congregate, bird waste soon collects. This bird waste, called *guano*, eventually formed huge mountains of mineral-rich fertilizer prized by gardeners and farmers all over Europe and elsewhere. So superior was it to other fertilizers that its high prices rescued the economy of the struggling nation of Peru.

The unpleasant task of working in the guano stations fell to the poorest Peruvians, usually Indians, who suffered terrible skin diseases and often went blind as a result of the ammonia fumes from the bird waste. Peru's economic potential from guano (as well as from cotton, sugar, and newly discovered copper) attracted the attention of foreign investors and governments, and for a while Peru seemed to be indeed on the verge of becoming a kind of El Dorado after all.

Income from guano and other crops ushered in a new period of development, characterized by the building of railroads, government-funded buildings, and other projects. However, eventually the mountains of bird waste were exhausted and the guano boom ended, bringing about a new economic crisis for the nation.

vians. It was now the 1920s, however, and around the world workers were beginning to organize unions and demand decent wages and working conditions.

In 1924 a Peruvian political activist, Víctor Raúl Haya de la Torre, founded the Alianza Popular Revolucionaria Americana, popularly known as APRA. Haya de la Torre advocated workers' and peasant farmers' rights and a stronger national government with broad powers to redistribute some of the wealth of Peru to benefit its poor. He advocated nationalizing key industries so that the government rather than individuals would own the companies that relied on Peru's natural resources or created essential products. He faced strong opposition from the current president-turned-dictator Augusto Leguía, who remained in power, in violation of the Peruvian constitution, until 1930. Haya de la Torre and another political leader, José Carlos Mariátegui, the founder of the Peruvian Socialist Party, were serious threats to the ruling military and civilian elite of Peru, though Mariátegui's leadership was lost when he died in 1930. Haya de la Torre ran for president in 1931, but lost amid widespread allegations of election fraud.

Other than for a brief period in the 1940s, APRA was forced to the sidelines by both civilian and military governments. By the 1950s APRA was seen by many, especially the young, as not radical or aggressive enough to take control of a Peru burdened by inflation, corruption, interference by international corporations, and civil unrest. In 1956 Francisco Belaunde formed a new group first called the National Youth Front and later renamed Acción Popular. He was narrowly defeated for president by the unlikely alliance of APRA and the army, a union that permanently undermined APRA's credibility as a party favoring reform. Belaunde's election loss caused him to rethink his positions, and after watering down his ideas, he was eventually elected president in 1963. However, his friendliness with foreign oil corporations seemed so contrary to his original reformist positions that he gradually lost support, and he was ousted in a bloodless military coup in 1968.

THE TURBULENT 1970S AND 1980S

Peru had not heard the last of either Haya de la Torre or Belaunde, however. Ironically, at first the leader of the coup that toppled Belaunde, General Juan Velasco, seemed a more effective and radical reformer than either Haya de la Torre or Belaunde. He made major, sweeping reforms, such as nationalizing the gas, mining, and fishing industries; expropriating large estates and turning them over to peasants to run as cooperatives; and recognizing Peru as a bilingual country. Before Velasco, Peru had one official language, Spanish, but under Velasco and up to the present day, it has two—Spanish and Quechua, the tongue of the Inca, spoken by the majority of Andeans.

Velasco's measures were well intentioned but not very practical. The country's finances were too precarious to risk costly reforms, and the leadership needed to make a success of the new cooperatives and nationalized industries was lacking. By 1975 much of the military no longer supported the general, and they staged a successful coup. By 1977 people had had enough of this new government as well, and in an atmosphere of civil unrest, strikes, and spiraling inflation, an open election was called. Haya de la Torre was elected president and served for three years. One of his final and most politically consequential acts was to grant the right to vote to millions of Peruvians earlier denied suffrage because of illiteracy. In the 1980 election that followed, Belaunde was returned to the presidency.

Belaunde's plans for Peru were too grand for the economic realities of the time. He soon had created a financial crisis of such magnitude that Peru was faced with the choice of defaulting on its international debt or abandoning his pet projects, such as building roads across the Andes into the Amazon Basin. Like others before him, he responded to his waning popularity first with empty rhetoric and promises and then with repression. Strikes were put down by riot police armed with tear gas and clubs, which only served to antagonize the voters of Peru even further.

Much had changed in the twelve years since Belaunde had been marched from the president's palace in his pajamas and sent into exile. People were frustrated by unrealized promises of change, leadership that was not up to the task, disastrous weather caused by El Niño, and worldwide economic recession that made it harder than ever to make strong financial strides. Added to their concerns was the terrorism of new radical groups, most notably the one known as Sendero Luminoso, or Shining Path.

SENDERO LUMINOSO

Sendero Luminoso, or Shining Path, was a secret society of ten to fifteen thousand followers of the communist philosophy of Mao Tse-tung of China. Sendero Luminoso was led by Abimael Guzmán, a former philosophy professor from Ayacucho who went by the name Comrade Gonzalo. Sendero's base was the poor peasants of Peru, particularly the Quechua speakers of the Andes. Gonzalo advocated terrorist acts against businessmen, police, and local officials; and sabotage of buildings, power lines, and petrochemical plants, particularly in the Lima and Ayacucho area, as a means of forcing the government to improve the living conditions of Peru's poor.

According to Jane Holligan, in her article "Democracy and Crisis" in *Insight Guide: Peru*, the Belaunde government "badly misjudged the Sendero Luminoso revolt in the Andes, ignoring early signs of activity, then allowing counter-insurgency forces to act with indiscriminate violence against the Indian population." More than three thousand peasants were killed by government troops in 1984, in a futile campaign to wipe out Sendero once and for all.

Sendero Luminoso was a major force in Peruvian politics for several decades, giving rise to other terrorist groups, most notably the Movimiento Revolucionario Tupac Amaru (MRTA), which took the name of the fabled Inca ruler. With its base in the slums of Lima, Tupac Amaru achieved international notoriety in the 1990s when it laid siege to the Japanese embassy, holding its three hundred occupants hostage for 126 days.

ALAN GARCIA

Belaunde lost the presidential election of 1985 to a young and charismatic member of APRA, Alan Garcia. Sendero Luminoso, funded in large part by the cocaine trade, continued its terrorist activities unabated, undermining Garcia's role as his country's leader. As Jenkins explains, "With Sendero proclaiming their revolution by 'teaching' and terrorizing peasant communities on the one hand, and the military evidently liquidating the inhabitants of villages suspected of 'collaboration' on the other, these years were a sad and bloody time for a large number of Peruvians."[24]

Growing discontent with the bloodshed in Peru, inflation running as high as 40 percent a month, embarrassment at failure to keep pace with international debt, and allegations of graft and corruption took their toll on Garcia's presidency, and he left office in 1990. According to Jane Holligan, "One of Garcia's legacies was the popular disgust with all traditional parties. That disillusion turned into a tidal wave of support for a former agricultural university rector, Alberto Fujimori."[25] The son of Japanese immigrants, Fujimori was perceived as one of the masses rather than a member of the wealthy ruling class or military. Fujimori and his Cambio (Change) 90 Party steadily gained support in the presidential campaign, as a clear contrast to what people considered to be the old-fashioned elitism of his opponent, noted writer Mario Vargas Llosa.

President Alberto Fujimori's leadership brought stability to Peru for a decade.

A NEW ERA

Alberto Fujimori was elected president in 1990. He proved to be a confident and gutsy leader, although many of his tactics were controversial. One of his first moves after his election was a risky package of price increases and currency devaluation, nicknamed Fujishock, which caused much hardship, especially for the poor. He remained popular despite such measures because people perceived him as doing what was needed to get the country back on track. Fujishock is credited with reducing annual inflation from 2,777 percent in 1989 to 10 percent in 1996. He took a second extraordinary step in 1992, when he declared an *autogolpe*, or self-coup, dissolving congress and the supreme court and giving himself much more power.

Later in 1992 he had another victory when Abimael Guzmán, alias Comrade Gonzalo of Sendero Luminoso, was captured. After that point Fujimori was widely felt to be the leader Peru so desperately needed, the right person at the right time, and his popularity skyrocketed at home and around the world. In 1995 he was reelected easily. Late in his second term, however, Fujimori's hold on power began to weaken.

THE FALL OF FUJIMORI

Fujimori's reputation as a reformer dedicated to doing whatever it took to solve problems contributed to his popularity at the beginning of his presidency. However, as years passed, Fujimori began to look more and more like a dictator. Though he had been able to sidestep the constitution on a technicality and get himself elected to a third term in 2000, there was evidence of election tampering in the first round, and the opposition boycotted the runoff. More and more evidence of violations of human rights during his antiterrorism campaign against Sendero Luminoso and other groups also surfaced during his campaign for a third term. Many Peruvians and others, including American Lori Berenson, were jailed after grossly inadequate trials on terrorism charges.

A woman holds a sign that reads "Go away dictator." Eighty percent of Peruvians approved of Fujimori's resignation.

Fujimori also no longer looked like an outsider to Peruvian politics as usual. Calling himself "the chosen guide . . . who knows the correct path"[26] for Peru, he appeared to many to be equating his own advancement and self-interests with the nation's. He tended to support wealthy foreign investors over Peruvians in the awarding of contracts and exploration rights for minerals, oil, and other natural resources, and had shown gross indifference to the deteriorating quality of life of poor Peruvians. Rather than a man of the people, he now looked to many like just another politician who favored the rich and powerful at the expense of the average citizen.

In fall 2000, the Fujimori-appointed head of the National Intelligence Service, Vladimiro Montesinos, was caught offering a bribe to an opposition party lawmaker in order to get him to change his vote on an issue important to Fujimori. Fujimori was unable to distance himself from Montesinos's actions, because such a clear violation of ethics and law seemed to the average Peruvian like something Fujimori would sanction. A further scandal erupted around the same time, when it was revealed that members of the Peruvian military had been involved in arms smuggling to Colombian guerrillas. A lackluster year for the economy also contributed to Fujimori's plummeting popularity across Peru.

In late 2000, Fujimori fired Montesinos; initiated a retrial of Lori Berenson, whose imprisonment had been a source of tension with the United States; and announced his resignation effective as soon as new elections could be conducted. Even this step was not enough to satisfy his critics. Polls indicated that 80 percent approved of his decision to leave office early, but mistrust of Fujimori ran so high by this point that the citizens of Peru were not willing to allow him to remain in power even for the six months it would take to conduct a new election. Fujimori flew to Japan, and while there, sent a letter of resignation, effective immediately, to the Peruvian legislature. Many saw this as the act of a coward unable to risk facing his countrymen, but most were simply relieved that Fujimori was finally gone. Still, the Fujimori era, despite the flaws, was the most stable of the twentieth century in Peru, and one of the most lasting on the entire continent in the last few decades.

DAILY LIFE IN PERU

4

Though the specifics of life in Peru vary greatly from region to region, for the vast majority of rural Peruvians, daily activities are essentially the same. They revolve around getting and preparing food, caring for family, educating children, and working outside the home. Getting food might involve setting out in a small boat to spear fish or scrambling across rocky terraces to tend crops. Educating the young involves teaching girls to cook and boys to tend crops, as well as sending them to school to learn to read. Working outside the home might involve holding down a job for which one is paid, or it might focus around taking care of one's own animals, and perhaps the neighbors' as well. Regardless of the activity and where it takes place, however, daily life largely revolves around doing what is necessary to survive. Still, there is some time to relax and be playful, and Peruvians have developed some unique and colorful ways to celebrate these occasions.

HOUSING AND COMMUNITIES IN THE ANDES

Although in recent decades better roads have made contact with the outside world slightly easier, life in the Andes goes on today much as it has for centuries. Individual homes still look much as they always have, usually consisting of adobe bricks (or in some regions of stone), dirt floors, and roofs either of tile or thatched grass. Homes usually have only one or two rooms, sometimes with a second story for food storage. A cooking fire dominates one corner. The rest of the space is almost devoid of furniture, which often consists of only a few stools. Lacking beds or even a table, the poorest families sleep on woolen blankets over sheepskins laid directly on the floor. People crouch to eat off mats on the floor. Slightly better-off families may own a table or a wooden bed frame and mattress stuffed with dried grasses, and occasionally the most prized possession of all—a radio. For the most part, however, possessions rarely go beyond clothing, bedding, pots and pans, and a few agricultural tools.

A typical Andes farmhouse is made of stone and has a dirt floor. These homes lack all modern conveniences including furniture.

Homes are clustered into villages and towns of two basic types. Villages organized around livestock herding, and cultivation of potatoes and other crops such as grains, tend to be small and widely scattered. This is because in the high-altitude region known as the *puna*, there is little arable land and grasses for grazing are sparse. The typical village consists of a small group of homes, next to corrals usually made of stacked stones in rings. Beyond the houses and corrals are small cultivated fields, and beyond that, sometimes at some distance, are the pasturelands and crops.

A second type of village has its origin in the *reducciónes*, the Spanish term for the new settlements formed by the forced relocation of many peasants during the *encomienda* period. Many of these villages today are not much larger than the more remote villages, but they are organized in a more typically Spanish style. The center of town is a square, or *plaza*, from which radiate cobblestone streets lined with houses. "And sometimes," according to author Pam Barrett, " in some town in the middle of nowhere, you will find a magnificent, rambling, adobe church, its tiled roof sagging, its gloomy interior still brightened by a great altar of tarnished silver or flaking gilt, its walls still adorned by enormous paintings, their ornate frames warped and their images darkened to obscurity by the years."[27]

GROWING FOOD

Daily life in the typical Andean town or village of either type revolves around growing and preparing food, but specific activities vary by the seasons. The agricultural season begins when winter draws to a close, which south of the equator is

COCA

Sixty percent of the world's coca crop, from which cocaine is derived, is grown on the slopes of the eastern Andes. Coca leaves have been used by Peruvians for four thousand years to ward off hunger and fatigue and to increase energy. Coca originally was condemned by the Catholic Church, but by the 1600s church leaders had changed their mind, once they discovered that the workers in the mines simply could not survive their brutal conditions without it. The Church's motives were not sympathy for the workers but profit: The Church charged a fee for every basket of leaves carried by caravan to the mines. Even today miners are some of the biggest users of coca leaves, but it is also commonly given to women in labor and chewed routinely by nearly anyone with access to a supply.

Coca was unknown in the United States and Europe until the mid–nineteenth century when a wine made from the leaf became popular. The original formulation of Coca-Cola contained coca (as is evident from the name of the beverage) before the long-range addictive qualities of the drug were clearly understood. Today huge amounts of coca are grown in Peru, where they are crushed by foot and converted into a paste that is sent to Colombia for pro-

cessing into cocaine. The dangers of cocaine befall not only its users, but also the growers themselves, who often find themselves in pitched gun battles with Peruvian drug squads and U.S. Drug Enforcement units, as well as with Colombian drug traffickers and political terrorists who want a cut of the action.

A Peruvian Indian prepares to make paste out of coca leaves. Tribal members use the paste to help them hunt for days with little food or rest.

in August or September. Fields to be planted must be hoed and weeded, and last year's fields must have the soil turned under to prepare them to rest fallow for a year. Usually only hand instruments such as hoes are used for these purposes, and the work is backbreaking and slow. Added to the misery is the fact that this work must be done in the rainy season. People slog through mud, pelted by rain and hail, to get their family lands tilled and planted, for at these altitudes the growing season is short and these tasks cannot wait.

Potato fields—which, unlike other arable land, are usually owned by the community and not by individuals—often lie several hours' walk from the village because they require less ongoing labor. Once the rains have ended, the potatoes can be harvested. Because this can take several weeks, it is not practical to go back and forth, so the whole village moves to the fields, leaving behind one family member per household to tend the animals. When the potato harvest is done, it is soon time to harvest the crops planted during the rainy season. When all harvests are finished, the crops are stored, with the goal of always having enough food to last until the next harvest, and enough surplus to survive another year if the crops should fail.

SCHOOL

Despite the fact that rural children are needed as workers, their education, at least to a point of basic literacy, is important to their families. According to Hudson, editor of *Peru: A Country Study*, "It is no exaggeration to say that the presence of a village school and teacher is considered by the poor as the most important first step on the road . . . out of poverty."[28] By 1988 there were approximately twenty-eight thousand primary schools in Peru—enough for almost every village of over two hundred people to have access to at least some formal education.

Schooling is largely devoted to learning to speak, read, and write Spanish. Despite the fact that Quechua, the language of the Andes, is acknowledged as one of the two official languages of Peru, it is looked down upon as a language of peasants, and social advancement and participation in politics or in the government requires knowledge of written and spoken Spanish. Andeans know this, and they see this part of their children's education as the key to improving their chances to live a better life.

The Ministry of Education in Lima oversees the network of schools, and though it provides textbooks and prescribes curriculum for all schools, it plays only a small role in the education of village children. The majority of *escuelitas*, or little schools, in small villages were not built by the government but by the villagers themselves and are maintained by local communities, with financial assistance from associations in Lima and other cities to which former villagers have moved. These associations raise funds to send to their hometowns for use in the schools and other community projects.

Opportunities for education beyond the primary grades are extremely limited for typical residents of rural areas. Although there are approximately fifty-four hundred secondary schools, or *colegios*, spread all over the country, and it is in fact required by law that all provincial capitals have at least one, few rural children ever receive a high school diploma. Those who do are held in extremely high esteem in their communities and are expected to be the voice of their people in political matters.

Children are taught to speak, read, and write in Spanish in Peruvian schools such as this one in Cuzco.

A TYPICAL DAY IN THE ANDES

Several months of the year, however, it is difficult for children to attend school at all because they are needed at home. During the growing season, the life of the whole family revolves around the necessity of getting enough food grown, harvested, and stored to ensure the family's survival. A day in the Andes during the growing season often begins before daylight with a cup of *mate*, a kind of herbal tea sweetened with sugar. *Mote*, a staple of the Andean diet consisting of dried corn reconstituted with boiling water, is often eaten for breakfast, although bread is also common. This first breakfast is very small, largely to hold off hunger until a larger breakfast can be prepared. Though called lunch, or *almuerzo*, it is eaten still fairly early in the morning, before the men set out for work in the fields. Typically it will consist of a soup or stew of potatoes and vegetables, and perhaps a second kind of potatoes. This will be served with pepper sauce and probably a glass of a corn beer called *chicha*.

At midday women bring a packed meal to the fields. If a man is being assisted by neighbors, his wife is expected to feed them as well, knowing that the favor will be returned when her husband helps out the neighbors in turn. As a show of appre-

THE *MINKA*

In the Andes, where hard physical labor consumes so much of daily life, several traditions have evolved to lighten the load. One of these is known in the Quechua language as *minka*. In a *minka*, relatives and friends of a family pitch in to help plant or harvest, but the mood is lighthearted as a result of the musicians who come along to entertain them. Plenty of food and drink are provided by the host, including *chicha* and *trago*. As a result of the alcohol in these two beverages, by midafternoon very little productive work is accomplished, although a good time is had by all. Because of the inefficiency of the *minka*, people who are concerned about getting a job done quickly and efficiently use *ayni*, another Quechua word for a system of direct exchange of labor between neighbors, and better-off farmers may even hire temporary workers. However, according to Rex A. Hudson in *Peru: A Country Study*, "the purpose of the *minka* is obviously social and communal as well as economic," and villagers enjoy the *minka* too much to let it die in the interests of efficiency.

ciation, this meal is the most elaborate of the day, consisting of several dishes, one of which will contain meat whenever possible. The wives of the men helping the family that day may or may not help prepare the meal and deliver it to the fields, depending on how pressing their obligations are at home. More *chicha* and a hard liquor called *trago*, made from sugar cane, will be brought as part of the meal, making it a rather leisurely affair shared by men and women alike. After this meal the women's main cooking responsibilities are done for the day, and they may stay to help in the fields or return home, depending on what other housework remains to be done.

All housework is considered suitable only for women. In addition to cooking, housework typically includes tending the small children, feeding the family chickens and pigs, and milking the family cow in the morning before an older child takes it and the sheep to pasture for the day. Women also take up and put down the bedding, sweep, do dishes, and perform all other household chores. The last chore of the day is preparing *mate* or perhaps a cup of warmed *chicha* to have before going to bed shortly after nightfall, to rest up for the long day ahead.

LIFE IN THE *SELVA* AND ALONG THE COAST

Although the details vary by location, the pattern of life is similar, and equally hard, for people living in other parts of rural Peru. Though estimates vary, less than 10 percent of the country's total population lives in the huge eastern watershed region of the *selva*, making it by far the most isolated part of Peru. The census identifies sixty-five different ethnic groups in the *selva*, and, according to Holligan de Diaz-Limaco, "while some have been contacted for years, live side by side with mainstream culture, and adopt modern dress, others have been seen only fleetingly and remain elusive."[29]

A typical settlement could be only a few huts along a riverbank or a community of several thousand, but regardless of size, life in rural Amazonian villages revolves around the river. As in the Andes, "there is little different in their lifestyle, apart from the arrival of schools, from that of . . . centuries before."[30] Riverbank houses are still built on stilts to accommodate the varying levels of the river and to provide some barrier against dangerous land animals that live in and along the water. Much of the diet is provided by fish caught by the men of the villages.

People of the *selva* also make use of the resources of the land. They supplement the fish in their diet with yucca, a root vegetable somewhat like a turnip, which grows wild but is also successfully cultivated. The yucca is boiled, then mashed and eaten as a paste. From yucca, people also make beverages, including one known as *masato* among the Ashaninka, one of the larger ethnic groups in the Amazon. *Masato* is a vivid pinkish-purple beverage, fermented to be mildly alcoholic, and is drunk by everyone, even babies. Many medicines are made from plants of the *selva*, and clothing, such as the Ashaninka tunic called a *kushma*, is made from plant fibers and colored with plant dyes.

Along the coast, life also revolves around fishing but also includes more extensive use of agriculture than is possible in the *selva*. Nevertheless the traditional patterns of life remain. Men are generally responsible for work outside the home, whether this means going off to fish in the reed boats known as *tortaras*, or irrigating and cultivating fields along the narrow, dry coastal strip. Women are responsible for home and family, and children's time is a mixture of chores and schooling.

POOR IN THE CITY

If life is difficult for the rural poor, it is downright brutal for those who live in the cities. Of Lima's nearly 8 million residents, more than half live either in shantytowns on the outskirts of the city or in slums in its center. Many concrete apartment blocks built in the 1950s to handle earlier waves of newcomers have become run-down eyesores today, but with their sewer systems, electricity, and running water, they are still an improvement over the residences of the shantytowns. Here, people build houses from whatever is available—bamboo, straw, packing materials such as cardboard, and bricks and other materials scrounged or stolen from construction sites. Basic services such as running water, toilets, and electricity are nonexistent in the shantytowns.

Daily life is hard for men and women alike. Additionally, many children die at birth or in early childhood because of unsanitary conditions or poor maternal health; those who live usually have little opportunity to enjoy childhood or get an education because their labor is required to ensure the family's survival. As Hudson points out, life in the shantytowns is "a constant scramble for existence."[31] Men often leave home before daybreak to make the long bus trip to constructions sites, which are the most typical place of employment for the newly arrived poor. They do things by hand that could be done more safely and easily by machinery, such as hauling buckets of cement up ladders or scaffolding. Because there are so many of them and they are paid so little, companies see no point in making the investment in machinery. Hard hats, steel-toed shoes, and goggles are rarely provided even for the most hazardous work, and injuries and deaths are common.

While the men are at work, the women haul water from taps that are often many blocks from their home. Lacking central electricity or gas, they cook over kerosene stoves. Whenever their labor can be spared, female family members try to find work as maids or in other low-paying, low-status positions, to supplement the wages of the men. Because of the difficulty and danger of life for the men, many women are either abandoned or widowed, and they must make ends meet entirely on their own. This creates an even greater hardship for families in the shantytowns.

A woman washes clothes outside her home in the slum district of Lima.

WEALTHY IN THE CITY

Well-to-do Peruvians generally tend to live in the coastal cities, and most of the wealthiest live in Lima. In addition to the rich, cities are home to a middle class made up of professionals such as doctors, teachers, engineers, and high-ranking government and military officials. While the wealthiest clearly live far more lavishly than those in the lower end of the middle class, the middle and upper classes share many values and spend their money on many of the same things.

Education, for example, is one of the ways a family gains social standing and prestige. Being able to send one's children to private school is a sign of status, and certain schools have more status than others. The very wealthy often send their children abroad to Europe or the United States for high school and university educations. European and American contact is particularly prized, and thus traveling to Europe, as well as to New York and places like Disney World, to shop for the latest fashions and to take vacations, also plays a significant role in enhancing one's social status.

Another sign of social status is one's home. The very rich may have several homes in Peru and abroad, but those of

THE HONORED PROFESSION OF TEACHING

For many years teachers were prohibited from holding public office because it was felt that, as with priests, the extraordinarily high esteem in which they were held would give them undue influence over their districts. According to Rex A. Hudson in *Peru: A Country Study,* "The power accruing to a teacher as the only person with post-secondary education in a small rural town can be considerable; the teacher is sought out to solve personal and village problems, settle disputes, and act as spokesperson for the community."

Teaching is considered a respectable profession for both men and women, but it is a particularly important occupation for women, who have fewer opportunities to pursue other prestigious careers. The high esteem in which teachers are held is in large degree due to Peruvians' general respect for educational achievement of any sort. People who have received advanced degrees in any field are called "doctor" as an honorary title, and completion of a degree is routinely announced in newspapers in Lima and elsewhere.

A private home, such as this one in Huaraz, is a sign of social status among the well-to-do.

lesser means strive to maintain a luxurious single residence. According to Hudson, "The home is prized and well cared for, with patios and yards protected by glass-studded walls and, in recent years, by electrical devices to keep out thieves."[32] In even the most modest middle-class homes, there are several servants, usually poor women from the barrios and shantytowns. Larger homes have servant quarters, and for many women the chance to get away from the poverty of their homes, even as poorly paid (and often abused) servants, is the greatest opportunity of their lives. Recent reforms have required employers to give servants the chance to go to school, and this has enabled many to learn trades such as cosmetology and tailoring, which enable them in time to quit domestic work and live independently.

Stories filter back to the coastal and mountain villages about those who succeed in making a better life for themselves in the city, prompting more people to come to Lima, Arequipa, and other cities. Just as many, however, are finding their way back home, their dreams dashed in the realities of the shantytowns. Frequently the homecoming is anything but easy. Children born in the city often find the monotonous routines of village life too dull, and even adults can find the readjustment difficult. Still, most people in Peru have realistic and very modest expectations for life. All they wish for is survival.

5

ARTS AND CULTURE IN PERU

On the day of the June solstice, which south of the equator signifies the beginning of winter, the Inca performed a traditional ritual of symbolically tying the sun to a stone in a festival known as Inti Raymi, the Festival of the Sun. Through dance, song, and offerings, the Inca tried to persuade the sun to stay in the sky longer, ushering in a new planting season and warming up their cold mountain world. After the Spanish conquest, Catholic missionaries, who considered elimination of all pagan rituals to be essential to saving the souls of indigenous people, tried without success to eliminate Inti Raymi. Eventually they decided a better approach was to weaken the festival's roots by combining it with the important feast day of John the Baptist, which occurred around the same time of year.

Inti Raymi is still celebrated across Peru today as a mixed Inca and Catholic holiday. The most famous and elaborate celebration is in Cuzco, the former Inca capital city. The formal celebration involves both a procession with Catholic icons from the village church and the sacrificial killing of a llama, a practice dating from Inca times. Afterwards music pours onto the streets from dozens of traditional and modern bands, and everyone dances, following either the specific formal steps of centuries-old dances or improvising to the latest tunes. People dress in traditional clothing or in their newest outfits, which in Peru are commonly called "clothes to dance in," and eat and drink until exhaustion forces them home to bed. Inti Raymi thus serves as perhaps the best single illustration of some basic truths about Peruvian culture: it is a fusion of past and present, of diverse ethnic and religious groups, and of many different art forms.

MUSIC

The vibrant results of this fusion are well illustrated in the music of Peru. According to Simon Broughton and the other editors of *World Music: The Rough Guide,* "Latin America's oldest musical traditions are those of the Andean Indians"[33] of today's Peru, Bolivia, and Chile, as well as parts of Ecuador and Argentina. Because the music of the Inca was not written down, it is not possible today to be sure exactly what its rhythms and vocals were like; but broken instruments similar to some still in use today have been found at ceremonial sites around the country and give at least some idea of how it must have sounded.

After the Spanish conquest, several other musical traditions began to blend with indigenous styles. Most notable among these are Spanish rhythms and instruments and African musical traditions brought by the slaves who accompanied the first settlers as servants and then were imported in large numbers to work the fields of the coast. In more recent

Women dressed in traditional clothing participate in a procession during Inti Raymi, an annual festival.

generations, other South American styles such as the *cumbia*, a Colombian dance rhythm, and American imports such as jazz and rap have also influenced Peruvian music.

TRADITIONAL MUSIC

Still, regardless of what kind of Peruvian music one listens to, from folk to top forty, the Andean roots are almost certain still to be clearly discernible. This influence is most evident in the instruments used, most notably the unique flutes, panpipes, and other woodwinds. Typical Andean flutes point down from the mouth rather than across the shoulder and are made of wood, or occasionally now of polyurethane tubing salvaged from building projects. Most are played in the same manner as a Western recorder, by blowing through the top and changing pitches by plugging or unplugging holes with one's fingertips. Panpipes are a series of three or more tubes lashed together to make one instrument. Each tube plays only one note, its pitch determined by the length of the tube. The tubes are closed at the bottom end, and the instrument is played by blowing across the top to set up a vibration. The performer's breath can be heard as part of the characteristic sound of the panpipes.

A Peruvian child holds a panpipe, an instrument used in traditional Peruvian music.

Most Andean woodwinds cannot play a wide range of notes. To make up for this, Andean performers are often highly skilled at moving between one instrument and another without losing track of the rhythm or pace of the music. They also have developed a technique whereby several performers are used to play all the notes of a composition. They move as required by the melody from one musician to another in such a seamless fashion that it sounds as if only one person is playing one instrument. Sometimes there may be a dozen or more musicians sharing a melody in this fashion, a feat much admired by musicians around the world.

Other traditional instruments include a conch shell horn; a small guitar called a *charango*, made of an armadillo or tortoise shell; various kinds of drums; and an Andean harp. The harp has thirty-six strings spanning five octaves and is often converted into a marching band instrument by being slung over one shoulder and played blind behind the harpist's back. Today

A NIGHT ON THE TOWN IN CUZCO

Whatever the size of the community, a night on the town in the Andes will involve music. In small villages there is likely to be only one place to go, and the musicians are likely to be whoever shows up. In cities such as Cuzco, however, the range of options is wide.

One way to appreciate the music of Cuzco is simply to go to a club and settle in for the evening. Many *conjuntos*, or musical groups, pass through a number of clubs each evening, playing a set in each one before moving on. As a result, a wide range of groups and styles can be heard without leaving one's chair. Other people prefer to barhop, going from venue to venue looking for groups they like. Some combine the two by getting up and following a favorite group as they make the rounds from bar to bar. Many of these roaming bands are self-taught, and their quality varies widely. Some play only to make a little money and have no pretensions about their musical skill. The point is to have fun, which is easy to do with such delightful music and easygoing people.

Some clubs, however, hire resident *conjuntos* and do not allow strolling groups. Many of these musicians are formally trained and serious about writ-

ing and arranging music in addition to performing it. Usually they perform both Andean standards and their own compositions, most of which borrow heavily from traditional Andean music. Many of these ensembles are highly paid, and some even end up touring abroad or producing recordings.

A group of musicians performs in Cuzco.

even groups purporting to play traditional music have often adapted to accommodate nontraditional instruments that blend well with the Andean style, such as acoustic guitars and even the occasional snare drum and electric guitar.

MUSICAL STYLES

Peruvian *conjuntos*, or musical groups, not only play instruments that show a mix of old and new; they also often sing and play in styles best described as updated traditional. The most typical style of the Quechua-speaking descendants of

OLD SONGS OF LOVE AND LONELINESS

In the years after the Spanish conquest, many Peruvian and Spanish people began writing about life in Peru. In some works, a number of song types still easily discernible in Peruvian music today were identified. Many of these were tied to activities such as livestock herding (appropriately called a *llamada*), work in the field, or victory in battle. A sixteenth-century chronicler named Waman Puma wrote down the words to a song of a type known at the time as a *huanca* or a *yaravi*. These words, reprinted in *Insight Guide: Peru*, by Pam Barrett, show the poetic depth of the songs of the Inca era.

> You were a lie and an illusion
> Like everything which is reflected in the waters.
> Perhaps we shall some day meet and be together forever.
> Remembering your smiling eyes, I feel faint;
> Remembering your playful eyes, I am near death.

What Barrett calls "the universal themes of love, loss, and loneliness" reflected in today's *huaynos* clearly have their roots in music and poetry of a far more ancient time.

the Inca is the *huayno*, rarely heard outside of the Peruvian Andes. Its lyrics are usually a mix of Spanish and Quechua, and its "buoyant, swinging rhythms . . . are deceptive, for the lyrics fuse joy and sorrow."[34] Broughton describes its "unmistakable dance rhythm" as "reminiscent of a hopped-up waltz, which once heard is not easily forgotten."[35] Its beat encourages dancing, usually including loud foot stomping and cries of "Mas fuerza! Mas fuerza!" or "Harder! Harder!"[36] *Huaynos* are often sung in a high nasal voice, which, for Western listeners, takes some getting used to. These vocals are accompanied by traditional instruments such as *charangos* and harps, as well as nontraditional ones such as clarinets and trumpets. Performance of *huaynos*, like so many other tradition-based compositions, is flexible and largely improvised around the instruments available and the skills of the players.

Another musical style, though not as old as the *huaynos*, is known as *musica criolla*. As the name Creole music implies, this style has its roots in the musical traditions of Spain and other parts of Europe. Primarily music of the coastal cities, the term has no precise meaning and is generally applied to any music whose roots seem to come more from outside than inside Peru. If a piece of music, for example, has elements of Spanish flamenco, Argentinean tango, or American fox-trot (nicknamed Inca-Fox), it would generally be classified as *musica criolla*. Other styles particularly popular among urban youth include *cholo*, favored by young Indians, and *mestizo*, favored by those of mixed ethnicity. Still bowing to tradition in some respects, these styles also reflect young people's desire to be different, and in many cases sound more like their counterparts in the United States and around the world.

CONTEMPORARY MUSIC

Even music thought of as contemporary in Peru is likely to be grounded in the past. Perhaps the best example of this is the music known as *chicha*. Named after the Andean beer served in the shantytown taverns of Lima, where this musical style evolved in the 1960s, *chicha* had become by the 1980s "the most widespread urban music in Peru."[37] Described by Broughton as "Andean tropical music," it is "a fusion of urban cumbia (local versions of the original Colombian dance), traditional highland huayno, and rock."[38] Most *chicha* groups have electric guitars and synthesizers as well as conga players and vocalists who also play percussion instruments. Well-known *chicha* groups include Los Demonios de Mantaro (The Devils of Mantaro), Los Shapis, and Belem.

Chicha music is favored by young Peruvians, who respond not only to its lyrics about love, relationships, alienation, and belonging, but also to the very strong political strains of much of the music. The hardship of being poor and exploited and of being a displaced Indian are common themes, as illustrated by these lyrics from Los Shapis' song "El Ambulante" (The Street Seller):

> Ay, ay, ay, how sad it is to live
> How sad it is to dream
> I'm a street seller, I'm a proletarian [member of the
>   working class]
> Selling shoes, selling food, selling jackets
> I support my home.[39]

SUSANA BACA

Most people outside Peru are familiar with Peruvian music only from the small groups of Andean woodwind performers who frequent tourist locales and festivals around the world. People in the know, however, are aware that Peru has one of the most vibrant musical scenes on the South American continent. Though few groups and soloists have established international reputations, one exception has been Susana Baca, who became an international celebrity as a result of her work with David Byrne. Byrne, formerly of the group Talking Heads, has a special interest in what is collectively called *tropicalismo* and has introduced many South American artists and musical styles to the world.

Susana Baca is an Afro-Peruvian interested in promoting recognition of the African influence on Peruvian rhythms, instruments, and musical styles. Her financial success has enabled her to establish and run the Instituto Negrocontinuo, whose aim is to encourage upcoming Afro-Peruvian musicians and others interested in incorporating black influences in their music. In a recent interview, reported by Dilwyn Jenkins in *The Rough Guide to Peru*, Baca comments that "as a child I was aware we had our own way of cooking, our music, our dances . . . but it was only in the 1960s that this was asserted in public. A lot of people until then had been silenced . . . ashamed . . . rejecting their past. But then it began to take on a positive hue."

Many credit Baca as instrumental in promoting this positive hue. Her beautiful, melodic voice is at its best in her intimate arrangements of Peruvian poetry, including such lines as these from "Beautiful Faces" by Tite Curet Alonso:

> The beautiful faces
>
> Of my dark race
>
> Are made of weeping
>
> Pain and suffering
>
> They are the truth
>
> That life challenges
>
> But they carry within
>
> So much love.

Susana Baca has been influential in promoting black influences in Peruvian music.

LITERATURE

Like Peruvian music, Peruvian literature reflects a blend of themes, mixing individual and personal stories of relationships with critical, often biting commentary about political and social injustice and the overall harshness of life in Peru. Peru's most famous writer is, without question, Mario Vargas Llosa. His earliest novels are strongly autobiographical and considered his best by most readers. They include *The Time of the Hero* (1962), a story about a schoolboy in a corrupt military academy; and *Aunt Julia and the Scriptwriter* (1977), "a grand and comic novel spiraling out from the stories and exploits of a Bolivian scriptwriter who arrives in Lima to work on Peruvian radio soap operas."[40] Other works such as *Conversations in the Cathedral* (1969) are highly praised by critics and scholars because of their many levels of structure underneath an apparently disjointed surface, but ordinary readers often find much of Vargas Llosa's work hard to follow.

Other well-known Peruvian novelists include Martín Adán, Ciro Alegría, and Alfredo Bryce Echenique. Martín Adán is best known for his poetic novel *The Cardboard House*, and Alegría is renowned for *Broad and Alien Is the World*, written in the 1970s about life in the Peruvian highlands. Alfredo Bryce Echenique is, next to Vargas Llosa, probably Peru's best living novelist. Bryce Echenique grew up among the wealthy elite of Lima but has spent most of his life in Europe. His fiction, such as *A World for Julius* (1992), is usually set in the world he knew as a child, focusing on what he considers to be the rather cruel society of those with far more money than love. Bryce Echenique is generally more esteemed abroad than in Peru, where few find much sympathy for the idea of the psychological poverty of the small privileged class of their country.

Little of the literature of Peru is written in Quechua, largely because the Spanish-speaking elite rather than the Andean peasants have produced the majority of Peruvians educated enough to become writers. José María Arguedas is one of the first to break in any fashion from this tradition. A *mestizo* whose first language was Spanish, he learned Quechua from the servants in his home and included Quechua songs and phrases in his best-known work, *All the Bloods* (1964). *All the Bloods* is a sweeping novel of life in the Andes, portraying a wide range of characters from Indian villagers to wealthy landowners. Arguedas was part of a group of writers known collectively as the *indigenistas*, which translates roughly as supporters of the indigenous. The *indigenistas* took as a common theme the moral superiority of peasants over the middle class and the wealthy, in the process elevating Quechua to a status as a language it had not enjoyed before. Nevertheless, to be published more easily, most contemporary writers choose to use Spanish even if they are bilingual. The most common exception is songwriters, who often write in Quechua if their music is meant to have a traditional feel.

By far the best-known twentieth-century Peruvian poet is César Vallejo (1892–1938), who, like Bryce Echenique, lived in Paris most of his life. His poems, focusing on themes of alienation, displacement, suffering, and loneliness, still "stun with their brilliance."[41] "Romantic, but highly innovative in style,"[42] Vallejo's best-known poems are collected in a volume called *Poemas Humanos* (Human Poems), which includes these lines:

> Beloved is the one with bed bugs
> the one who has worn out shoes in the rain . . .
> the one who slams a finger in the door
> the one who has no birthday . . .
> the one of pure misery, the poor poor.[43]

VISUAL AND DECORATIVE ARTS

Peru is a nation not just of musicians and writers, but of other kinds of artists as well. Typical of all the arts in Peru, the visual and decorative arts are heavily influenced by traditions, some of them thousands of years old. In fact, some of the finest forms of contemporary Peruvian art are achieved in precisely the same media that the Moche and other vanished cultures developed and perfected long before the arrival of the Spanish: weaving, pottery, and metalwork. Others show clearly the influence of Christian church art but have been transformed to reflect Peruvian ideas of beauty, such as angels with Indian faces or statues of the Virgin Mary dressed as a Peruvian woman.

Peru has been particularly well known for centuries for its beautiful textiles, including cloth, weavings, and knitted goods. Wool from sheep, llama, and alpaca are typically used for weaving, although cotton is common as well. The hot pinks, vivid oranges, bright blues, and other colors associated with Peruvian fabrics are achieved by natural dyes perfected over the centuries. Colors and patterns often have symbolic meaning or associations with particular holidays or regions. Though some Peruvians are still careful to wear only

THE WEAVERS OF TAQUILE

In the middle of bright blue Lake Titicaca, on the Bolivian border, lies the island of Taquile. In a country known for its colors and vibrant ethnic traditions, Taquile is perhaps the most vivid sight in all Peru.

Taquile is known not only for cloth produced on looms, but also for knit garments and embroidered fabrics. According to Pam Barrett in *Insight Guide: Peru,* "The Taquile weaving cooperative is renowned for the quality of its garments, and the people habitually look as if they are dressed for a fiesta." The women dress in layered skirts, each of which is multicolored, and wear brightly colored blouses with embroidered trim. The traditional simple black shawl that covers their head only serves to accent the bright hues of the rest of their clothing. Men wear colored vests and black pants, topping off their outfits with brightly colored knit caps.

Textile production on Taquile, unlike many other places in Peru, is not considered only women's work. Men knit their own caps, and many produce knitted items for sale, while women tend to focus on weaving and sewing. At fiesta times, such as Santiago in July or Pacha Mama (Mother Earth) in August, the skill of the weavers of Taquile is especially evident in elaborately embroidered and decorated hats they save for these occasions.

Taquile is admired by many in the region for its farsightedness in setting its own terms for tourism. The number of visitors is strictly regulated, and no hotels have been allowed. People come on boats operated by villagers, and if they stay the night it is in a villager's home for a fee. The residents of Taquile know the value of their products and the charm of their island, and they are determined to use both to their advantage well into the future.

Two traditionally dressed Taquile natives knit wool caps.

colors they consider appropriate, many produce textiles for sale to tourists and city dwellers, who often do not have any idea of these associations. As a result, over time the richness of the symbolism has faded.

Textiles of remarkable beauty are seen everywhere in Peru. Mothers swaddle babies in wide blanketlike straps of brightly woven cloth, then secure them tightly in slings that are tied around the neck and shoulders. Skirts may be embroidered or layered to produce a riot of color. Hats are a particular focus for the skill of Peruvian knitters and handiworkers. Special hats are worn on holidays, and a person is as likely to be known by the hat he or she wears as by a regional accent.

Pottery and ceramics are also common art forms in Peru, and some art historians claim that the ceramics of the Moche and other groups have never been surpassed. Ceramic objects include brightly painted dishes, elaborate models of churches painted with designs, and other pieces designed for display in the homes of tourists who want souvenirs of their time in Peru.

One particular kind of decorative art at which Peruvians excel is the *retablo*. Brought by the Spanish to the New World, the *retablo* is a set of religious figurines usually of wood, papier-mâché, or clay. Small enough to be packed into a special hinged box, these figures could be easily unpacked by people on the

Peruvian objects made of precious metals, such as this gold Chimu funerary mask, are highly prized for their quality and detail.

move to serve as a shrine for prayer. Peruvian artisans soon adapted this art form to their preferred materials. Scenes often appear inside hollowed-out gourds, for example, and the finest Peruvian *retablo* figures are delicately carved in Huamanga stone, a beautiful white-and-gray material called Peru's marble. The *retablo's* original use as a portable shrine is still apparent today, for most *retablo* scenes continue to be of such events as the nativity. Nevertheless, today's artisans have fun making nontraditional statements in their *retablos*, including drunken revelers, naughty children, and other such figures in their finished works.

Beautifully detailed earrings such as these are worn by even the poorest villagers on special occasions.

A GOLDEN LEGACY

Though Peruvian arts are distinct and many have long histories, there is no art form that surpasses Peruvian metalwork. Jewelry and decorative objects by Peruvian artists working in gold, silver, and copper are among the most prized objects in the world. Peru has a long history of greatness in this area, dazzling early Spanish visitors with such masterpieces as the courtyard of the Temple of the Sun, which contained a life-size rural scene in solid gold, down to small details such as butterflies and cornstalks. In areas where precious metals are mined today, even poor villagers are often adorned on special occasions with intricate earrings and other beautiful jewelry. Most of the designs are derived from traditional patterns, but creative designers are always willing to try new things, especially now that international markets are growing for their work. Jewelry and other objects today may combine precious stones and metals with more everyday materials such as handpainted ceramic beads, creating one-of-a-kind works receiving worldwide acclaim for their beauty and originality.

As with music and other art forms, though Peruvians are more than willing to borrow what they like from Spanish and other cultures, they have never lost sight of what is uniquely theirs.

Toward a Truly Shining Path: Challenges of Contemporary Peru

The modern nation of Peru faces a number of formidable challenges in the twenty-first century. Many of these are tied in one way or another to the economy. Externally, Peru must improve its position as a trading power, and thus as a vital political power, in South America, the Pacific Rim, and the world. Closer to home, it must establish a more solid base of manufacturing and agricultural production within its own country, but must at the same time take steps to halt the environmental destruction that has come about as a result of the manufacturing and agricultural practices of the past. Most importantly, Peru must address the problem that seems to permeate everything about life in the country: the poverty of most of its citizens. In one way or another, this issue seems to be at the heart of most of the problems of the nation today and must be addressed if the future of Peru is to be better than its present.

Money Whitens

A common expression in Peru today is "money whitens." This expression has many different shades of meaning. First, it refers to the fact that although the elite of Peru are predominantly fair-skinned Europeans, economically successful *mestizos* and others are accepted into higher levels of society without apparent prejudice, even if their appearance is decidedly un-European. Their money, in other words, makes them white. The expression also means, however, that those *mestizos* and others who are well-off tend to forget their roots, losing interest in addressing the woes of the people from which they came.

The chasm between rich and poor, and the common desire of the middle class to be more like the *criollos*, or Peruvians of European ancestry, has created a situation where those who might be in a position to address the problems of the lower classes are often not willing to invest their time and energy in the effort. This is especially true if they feel that improving the lives of the poor might take away some luxury from their own lifestyle. It is this indifference that keeps millions of people living without even basic sanitation in shacks outside Lima. It is this indifference that maims and kills workers in work site accidents. It is this indifference that permits cholera and influenza epidemics to sweep through shantytowns, killing children and the elderly with particularly cruel efficiency.

There are, of course, many private citizens and politicians who see narrowing the gap between rich and poor, and creating more opportunities for the poor to improve their lives, as essential to the nation's future. However, the economy of the nation is founded on the labor of what seems to be an inexhaustible supply of people desperate enough to put up with anything to survive, and it is this situation that makes each of these workers seemingly expendable as an individual, and the fate of their families a matter of little interest to those in power. There is, in other words, little real economic incentive to change the situation as long as able-bodied men keep showing up at construction sites and mines and young girls knock on villa doors to enter service as domestic servants.

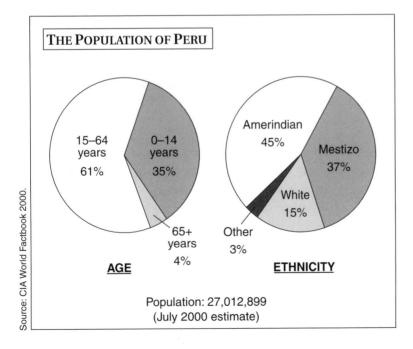

THE POPULATION OF PERU

15–64 years 61%

0–14 years 35%

65+ years 4%

AGE

Amerindian 45%

Mestizo 37%

White 15%

Other 3%

ETHNICITY

Population: 27,012,899
(July 2000 estimate)

Source: CIA World Factbook 2000.

HEALTH ISSUES

In Peru approximately 90 percent of rural residences and 25 percent of urban residences do not have a safe source of water or any kind of sewer or other system for handling waste. Unsafe drinking water and exposure to untreated waste cause many people to become sick and sometimes die of diseases such as gastroenteritis and malaria. Lack of access to safe water creates a generally unhygienic situation in which to live and contributes indirectly to many other diseases, such as respiratory infections, tuberculosis, influenza, measles, chicken pox, and whooping cough. According to Hudson, "In a typical case, during one year in Huaylas District, which had a small clinic and often was fortunate to have a doctor in residence, 40 percent of all deaths registered were children below four years of age, who died because of a regional influenza epidemic." In fact, even a cholera epidemic in the 1990s, severe enough to make international headlines, killed far fewer people during its course than did other diseases that are "endemic [prevalent], and thus taken for granted."[44]

Hardest hit by infectious diseases are those in rural areas and in the outlying shantytowns of the cities. Lima (excluding the shantytowns), for example, has a doctor for every 400 residents, other coastal regions average one per 2,000 residents, and the Andean highlands have one doctor per 12,000 residents. Similar discrepancies exist in the number of hospital beds, nurses, and all other aspects of health care. Lack of access to medical care, and to such related services as family planning, nutrition programs, and basic dentistry, has a direct negative impact on the health of the poor. Infant mortality, one of the best measures of the overall health of a nation, is lower than it used to be, but is still twice that of Colombia to the north and Chile to the south, exceeding all other countries in the western hemisphere except Bolivia and Haiti.

ENVIRONMENTAL ISSUES

The cholera epidemic and other health problems in Peru were (and are) in part due to the environmental degradation that has accompanied uncontrolled industrial growth and massive, unplanned migration to the cities. Air and water pollution in the urban areas, particularly Lima, has grown enormously as a result of dumping of industrial and other waste, as well as from motor vehicle exhaust. People have

ECOTOURISM

As more and more of the rain forest falls to opportunists seeking to gain quick fortunes from its resources, a counterforce is growing in strength. This movement is known worldwide as ecotourism. Ecotourism refers to programs that bring tourists to a region in a manner that has minimal negative impact on the area and provides opportunities to educate them about habitat preservation and sound ecological practices. Ecotourists do not expect the luxurious lodges of many game preserves, for these use a great deal of energy and create mounds of trash and other waste. From simple lodging, ecotourists set out, usually on foot or by small boat, to view wildlife and perhaps to interact with local people. Because ecotourism involves exhausting trips to remote places and is usually quite expensive, it appeals only to a small number of travelers, which is in fact necessary if it is to serve its purpose.

The Parque Nacional Manu in Madre de Dios is one of the world-premiere destinations for ecotourists. Called "the most bio-diverse rainforest park in

the world" by Pam Barrett in *Insight Guide: Peru,* Parque Nacional Manu is home to thirteen species of monkeys alone, as well as giant otters, capybaras, tapirs, jaguars, and over a thousand species of birds.

In the Amazon rain forest, an Indian examines a tourist's beard.

trouble breathing the choking air of Lima, and the water they drink contains toxins and other substances that undermine health and quality of life. In the coastal city of Chimbote, Hudson writes, "the lack of . . . basic services, absence of attention to environmental impacts, and totally inadequate municipal budgets led directly to converting Chimbote Bay, the best natural port on Peru's coast, into a cesspool of industrial and urban waste, meters thick in places."[45]

In rural areas, activities such as the establishment of huge illegal coca plantations along the eastern slopes of the Andes have also had devastating effects on the ecology. Perhaps the worst of these practices is a system of gold mining that involves bulldozing large stretches of rain forest and piling the gravel and soil onto special machinery that washes it with a solution containing mercury, a toxic metal used to separate out the gold. The process leaves horrible scars on the land and poisons the soil and water. Watershed

"WE ARE NOT LIKE THOSE FROM OUTSIDE"

The Rough Guide to Peru, by Dilwyn Jenkins, reports this testimony from an Amarakaeri Indian from the Amazon Basin, given recently to a human rights organization in Lima:

> We Indians were born, work, live and die in the basin of the Madre de Dios River of Peru. It's our land—the only thing we have, with its plants, animals, and small farms: an environment we understand and use well. We are not like those from outside who want to clear everything away, destroying the richness and leaving the forest ruined forever. We respect the forest; we make it produce for us.
>
> Many people ask us why we want so much land. They think we do not work all of it. But we work it differently from them, conserving it so that it will continue to produce for our children and grandchildren. Although some people want to take it from us, they then destroy and abandon it, moving on elsewhere. But we can't do that; we were born in our woodlands. Without them we will die.
>
> In spite of journeys to Puerto Maldonado to demand guarantees from the authorities, they do not support us by removing the people who invade our land. On the contrary, when we defend our land, forcing the invaders to retreat, they accuse us of being wild, fierce, and savage.
>
> We are not opposed to others living in and benefiting from the jungle, nor are we opposed to its development. On the contrary, what we want is that this development should benefit us, and not just the companies and colonists who come from outside. And we want the resources of the jungle to be conserved so that they can serve future generations of both colonists and Indians.

from the eastern Andes forms the Amazon Basin. In recent years the water of the basin has become laden not only with mercury from the mines, but also with pesticides and herbicide spray residues from the coca plantations, creating problems for fish and other Amazon life. This inevitably creates problems for the people who rely on the river for their food. Additionally, the practice of clear cutting, removing all vegetation from a stretch of rain forest in order to plant crops, has contributed to erosion, which dumps tons of mud into the rivers and streams. Animals and plants that require clear water to survive are choked off by the silt, and their loss diminishes the indigenous people's food sources. Though a new penal code for Peru, unveiled in the early 1990s, treats acts of environmental degradation as crimes and imposes stiff penalties, the new code has proven difficult to enact and enforce.

Urban sprawl is another ecological issue with long-range social effects. Peru has very little land that is easy to farm, and thus the flat coastal strip is especially important as a source of food for Peru's people and as part of the country's export economy. In recent years, major population shifts away from the Andes toward the coastal cities have resulted in more and more of this land being claimed for housing, and more and more of it ruined for agricultural use by pollutants. This is a particularly severe problem for Peru, because it already produces far less food than its people require, and it has become increasingly reliant on the United States and other countries to supply foreign aid in the form of food staples such as grain.

PROTECTING THE RIGHTS OF INDIGENOUS PEOPLE

The overall ecology of a region and the quality of life for human beings are closely linked. In Peru there has been little consideration given to either the environment or the people affected by ecologically disastrous practices. Early laws such as the 1974 Law of Native Communities were designed to clarify that indigenous groups owned their traditional lands, but such efforts have had a downside. Lands not clearly belonging to any group were then considered up for grabs by multinational corporations and others wishing to extract natural resources, such as gold and rubber, and to search for oil and natural gas.

Other laws seem to give lip service to the needs and rights of indigenous peoples while in fact working to their detriment, and some are thought by many to be steps backward. In 1995 President Fujimori signed a bill saying that any indigenous group that had "abandoned" its land for two years no longer could claim a right to it. Because many Amazonian cultures are nomadic, they appear to abandon land to which they in time return, and this law has been the source of conflict in the region.

INVOLVING RURAL PERUVIANS IN NATIONAL LIFE

Indigenous Peruvians from all regions are beginning to realize that they must become more involved in the life of the nation if they are to keep harmful laws and practices from undermining them further. Coming out of their isolation, however, has a downside as well. Contact with the outside world exposes indigenous cultures to influences that tend to weaken their traditions. Traditional dress gives way to T-shirts and plastic sandals, and traditional music gives way to portable radios. Often younger people leave the hardships of their communities behind to seek what usually ends up being a false dream of success in the city. Families may find themselves abandoned by fathers and husbands, who often intend either to come back with their earnings or send for their families later, but sometimes simply do not return. This has resulted in an erosion of traditional family structures and an increased burden on women to fulfill both their own roles and those of the absent spouse.

The introduction of primary schooling also has had a major effect on rural life. Generally, schooling is seen as a good thing, because when literate children grow up, they will have more opportunity to become involved in politics and government, to the benefit of their communities. But school also can undercut ethnic identification. In addition to meeting the goal of basic literacy, school is the place where a sense of national identity is consciously and deliberately formed. According to Hudson, "If nothing else, the primary school pupil learns that he or she is a Peruvian and that many of Peru's national heroes were martyred by Chilean [and Ecuadorian] forces against whom one must be constantly on guard."[46] In this way, along with other lessons to promote national pride, rural children are encouraged to see themselves not primarily as members of an indigenous group, but as part of a proud national Peruvian culture they must be

A Peruvian Indian woman registers to vote at a polling station outside Lima. Rural Peruvians are learning the value of having a voice in their government.

prepared to defend against internal and external threats, real or imagined. This emphasis on a Peruvian identity is seen by the government as essential to creating a unified country, but the net effect over the generations has been to treat indigenous cultures and local traditions as inferior and to downplay their importance in rural children's lives.

Nevertheless, most rural people today believe that the answer to their problems is not isolation, because it is clear that they will not be left in peace as long as there is something of value to be gotten from their land. A number of groups have sprung up to fight for indigenous rights, including the Inter-Ethnic Association for the Development of the Peruvian Amazon (AIDESEP) and the Confederation of Nationalities of the Peruvian Amazon (CONAP). These groups have active presences in Lima and the provincial capitals, where they lobby for and against proposed legislation, and they also serve as spokespeople for their communities when outsiders come to the region to do business.

THE ECONOMY

The arrival of outsiders wanting to set up businesses in Peru has been a major unsettling influence on the country in the last few decades. Outside investors, such as multinational mining and oil companies as well as other large manufacturers of consumer goods and machinery, use their own funds to develop industry

THE GROWING POWER OF WOMEN

Archaeological records from the Inca and previous cultures show that women had many of the same rights as men in those societies. However, the Spanish brought with them a culture often described as *machista*, in which women took a subservient role to men, finding their identity largely in their roles as wives and mothers. Things remained this way until the 1980s, when many men were forced from their homes by economic factors or killed by Sendero Luminoso, and women were forced to become the leaders of their homes and communities. Statistics show that 78 percent of migrant families in the 1980s were headed by women.

Though life was particularly hard for these women, many feel some good came of these hardships. In shantytowns such as those in Lima, women

formed Vaso de Leche (Glass of Milk) social clubs to provide breakfast to children. They organized community soup kitchens to ensure everyone's family was fed. Buoyed by their newfound strength as community organizers and leaders, women began running for political office, winning thirteen of 120 congressional seats in 1995. Martha Chavez was elected president of congress that same year.

Though women have made impressive political gains, the society remains quite chauvinistic, especially in rural areas, where women shoulder far more than their share of the burden of work and are far more likely to be illiterate. Still, for those in urban areas, the college attendance rate is almost equal between the two genders, and women are starting to assume roles as judges, professors, bankers, and business executives.

Women gather for an equal rights demonstration in Cuzco in 1994.

in Peru. Because Peru does not itself have the money for such projects, this might seem on the surface to be a good thing. However, it has been problematic because these companies are so rich that they can in some respects dictate to the government how they will do business, and thus they often behave irresponsibly in regard to the environment and the people of Peru. Also, large corporations often have a negative effect on smaller businesses, who find it difficult to compete. Individual shoemakers, for example, might find themselves unable to sell shoes at the same price as a large shoe factory, and thus either close down or be discouraged from opening businesses in the first place.

The various Peruvian governments' attitudes toward foreign investment have fluctuated wildly, as have many other economic policies, resulting in instability in both politics and the economy. In fact, presidential hopefuls often win elections based on their vow to implement radical change from whatever is the current practice, and this is likely to continue to cause instability for years to come. For example, export and import policies have swung back and forth between encouraging free trade, as they did under Fujimori, and discouraging it, as they did under several previous presidents, including Alan Garcia. The philosophical difference at the heart of these two strategies lies in whether it is a good idea to give an artificial boost to Peruvian businesses by taxing imported products so heavily that people could only afford to buy Peruvian ones. Heavy import taxes would encourage small businesses and force Peru to develop large industries such as computer companies and car and machinery manufacturers, something it very much needs to do to develop its overall economy. However, such policies are usually met by equally restrictive policies in the countries to whom Peru exports products. The net effect is that Peru loses the chance to bring new money into its economy by selling products abroad, new money the government desperately needs to provide social services, repair roads, and give incentives to farmers and others to improve their productivity. The question of whether to build a stronger economy by recycling money that is already within Peru or try to draw in outside money, perhaps at the expense of Peruvian businesses, is one to which there is no easy answer.

Differences in attitudes toward the government's role in developing the economy have been at the heart of many of the swings in policy that have destabilized Peru in recent decades. In 1968 President Velasco nationalized the International Petroleum Company's (IPC) holdings in Peru, setting in motion a number of changes in the nation's economic structure. Nationalization refers to the process by which a country rescinds a company's right to do business privately and takes over operation of the company itself. This was an immensely popular move because the IPC had become a target for people's resentment of the close (and mutually profitable) cooperation between previous presidents and foreign investors, a relationship that tended to make a few people richer and the vast majority poorer.

Nationalized companies function under direct government control so as (at least in theory) to turn the profit over to the people in the form of a larger national budget to build schools and hospitals, provide better social security programs, and improve transportation and other services. However, because companies being nationalized must be compensated for the value of the company they are losing, government buyouts are extremely expensive; and unless the nationalized industry makes a substantial profit, the country takes a huge economic loss in the process. Unfortunately, nationalized companies rarely run as efficiently and therefore as profitably as privately owned ones, and subsequent Peruvian presidents ended up selling many of the nationalized companies back to private investors.

Before the problems of nationalization were clearly understood, it seemed to be a way of taking from the rich and giving to the poor, something most Peruvians think is desperately needed. Other strategies to accomplish this, such as breaking up the huge *haciendas* of wealthy landowners and creating collective farms run by the local peasants themselves, were equally welcomed. Though many social scientists agree that in the long run the effect of this effort was a positive one because it broke the tradition of landownership by only a few, the collective farms did not work. Peasants had little business experience to draw on as managers, and most ended up paying little attention to their collective holdings and simply spent their time tending their private plots as they always had. Today the strategy is to help individual farmers make their lands more productive, rather than trying to get them to change their tradition of small family farms.

THE SHADOW ECONOMY

Traditional ways are at the heart of one of the great economic challenges of contemporary Peru: getting control of what economists call the informal sector. The term refers to those businesses and activities that take place outside of official places of employment. Also called the shadow economy,

This man participates in the shadow economy of Peru by selling his produce on the street.

these informal activities range from sitting on a corner to sell vegetables from one's garden, to bringing jeans or compact discs across the border in a suitcase and selling them for a profit, to flying a plane full of coca paste to Colombia for processing into cocaine. Though these activities vary widely in all other respects, what they have in common is that they operate outside of government control. One of the things Velasco hoped to accomplish by nationalization was to bring more of the economic activity under the watchful eye of the government, in part so it could be better regulated, but to a large degree so it could be taxed as a means of enlarging the grossly inadequate national budget.

For the typical Peruvian, poor and often displaced from his or her traditional home, the informal economy is the only beneficial one. They do not hold official jobs, instead arriving at work sites as day laborers and disappearing when the work is done. Having little money, they survive on barter of labor and goods, and on a strong tradition of community assistance. Those who own tiny businesses, such as operating an ice-cream cart or doing tailoring out of their home, see no advantage in making their business known to authorities, and often deliberately try to avoid detection. Those who participate in illegal activities, of course, are especially careful to remain hidden.

As a result, the standard measures of the economy of any country—such as its gross domestic product, its ratio of imports to exports, and its per capita income—are only part of the picture in Peru. The most dramatic example of this is the impact of coca on the overall economy. Moral issues aside, it is unquestionably true that, as Hudson points out, "If coca production were to fall back to traditional levels of consumption by Andean peasants themselves, many Peruvians would lose income."[47] Just how much income and how many people would be affected is unknown, but if coca profits were factored into the Peruvian economy, the gross domestic product (GDP) would rise somewhere between 4 to 7 percent. Figures for 1989 show that without coca, commodity exports to the United States alone were approximately $3.7 billion and with coca they were $5.6 billion. Clearly, getting control of at least this aspect of the shadow economy is more than a moral or social issue. It is also a major economic one; and though no one is seriously arguing that the Peruvian government should become involved in the cocaine trade as a way of making money, it is apparent that illegal trafficking in coca is having a major negative effect on Peru politically, environmentally, and socially. As long as peasants of

Sewing is just one of many paying jobs Peruvians pursue at home, away from the watchful eyes of the government.

LORI BERENSON

On November 30, 1995, Peruvian authorities arrested a young American journalist, Lori Berenson, on charges of terrorism. She was accused of being deeply involved with the organization known as the Movimiento Revolucionario Tupac Amaru (MRTA), commonly called Tupac Amaru, who had carried out an attack on congress and the takeover of the Japanese embassy earlier that year. After a sham trial in 1996 by a group of hooded military judges, Berenson was taken to a prison high in the Andes where she lived until late in 2000, sleeping on bare stone with only light blankets and receiving inadequate food and clothing.

She was then brought back to Lima to stand trial again, in an effort by President Fujimori to smooth over relations with the United States. President Clinton had made it clear that American funding of Peru's antidrug effort was in jeopardy if Berenson did not get a trial conducted in accordance with international standards of law. She has consistently proclaimed her innocence, claiming that her contact with Tupac Amaru was appropriate for a journalist trying to get a story. Peruvians as a whole do not believe her, and over half of those polled in late 2000 oppose her getting a new trial. Many were victims of the terrorism of the recent

past, and they do not sympathize with anyone they feel helped terrorists in any way. They feel strongly that her life sentence was deserved, and that she does not deserve any special treatment as an American citizen. Even after the trial, the full truth about Berenson will undoubtedly remain known only to herself. At any rate, political commentators see the new trial as being less about Berenson and her activities than it is about Fujimori and his. Fujimori has been widely accused of violating human rights as well as his country's own laws in his handling of terrorism.

Lori Berenson is escorted by Peruvian police to a reenactment of her alleged crime.

the *selva* feel there is no other, or better, way to make money legally, the focus will continue to be on coca, and the problems it causes for Peru will continue.

CURBING VIOLENCE AND TERRORISM

One of the problems resulting from drug trafficking is violence. Though such activities tend to breed violence in and of

Despite the long path ahead of them, Peruvians have the resources and the hope necessary to face the challenges of the twenty-first century.

themselves, the problem has been particularly acute in Peru in recent years because of the involvement of Sendero Luminoso, or Shining Path. Many of the activities of this group and others were funded through profits from drug trafficking, and Sendero Luminoso's tactics against the ethnic groups such as the Ashaninka, who live in the coca-producing region, were particularly ruthless and deadly. As a means of ensuring they could operate without local constraint, Sendero Luminoso killed many of the region's young men and forced an exodus to cities such as Lima, aggravating population problems there.

With the arrest in late 2000 of one of the last remaining leaders of Sendero Luminoso, it appears as if one positive legacy of Alberto Fujmori's time in office may be to have brought terrorism under control in Peru. Still, the problems of social inequity that gave rise to this group and others such as the Movimiento Revolucionario Tupac Amaru (MRTA) have not been addressed. As memories of recent horrors fade, other groups advocating sweeping away injustice by whatever means necessary may once again find many Peruvians sympathetic to their cause. Rural Peruvians are angry that what meager funds for social services are available are disproportionately spent in the cities, and poverty-stricken Peruvians are angry that not enough has been done to create the upward mobility that would close the gap between rich and poor. Indigenous Peruvians are angry at what they perceive as the pillaging of their land and resources and undermining of their culture by self-interested outsiders.

Indeed, there is a great deal to be angry about in Peru, and situations change quickly. In one week, for example, President Fujimori went from being newly elected to a third term to announcing his resignation. His inability to survive the controversies surrounding him was linked in part to Peruvians' views that Fujimori was standing in the way of progress. Many feel a new direction for Peru is needed, but these sentiments have caused the country to lurch from one inadequate answer to its problems to another. However, Peruvians have not given up hope that there may actually be a shining path for them in their future, although it will take all of them to achieve it. Pulling together as a nation will, in fact, be the defining challenge of the twenty-first century for this "pauper on a throne of gold."

Facts About Peru

Government

Country name: República del Perú/Republic of Peru

Government type: constitutional republic

Capital: Lima (population 7.6 million)

Administrative divisions: 24 departments

Independence: July 28, 1821

Executive branch:

  President: elected by popular vote to a five-year term

  Cabinet: appointed by president

Legislative branch: Unicameral (one house) Democratic Constituent Congress; 120 seats with members elected by popular vote for five-year terms

Judicial branch: Supreme Court appointed by National Council of the Judiciary

Geography

Area: 1,285,220 square kilometers

Bordering countries: Bolivia, Brazil, Chile, Colombia, Ecuador

Climate: varies from tropical to desert and from temperate to frigid, depending on location

Terrain: western coastal plain (*costa*), central high mountains (*sierra*), and eastern jungle (*selva*)

Elevation extremes: sea level to 6,768 meters (Nevado Huascarán)

Natural resources: copper, silver, gold, petroleum, timber, fish, iron ore, coal, phosphate, potash, hydropower

Land use:

  Arable land: 3%

  Pastures: 21%

  Forests/woodlands: 66%

  Other: 10%

Natural hazards: earthquakes, tsunamis, flooding, landslides, volcanic activity (mild)

Environmental issues: deforestation, overgrazing, desertification, air pollution, water pollution

PEOPLE

Population: 27,012,899 (July 2000 estimate)

Age structure:

    0–14 years: 35%

    15–64 years: 61%

    65+ years: 4%

Population growth rate: 1.75%

Birth rate: 24.48 births/1,000 population

Death rate: 5.84 deaths/1,000 population

Infant mortality rate: 40.6 deaths/1,000 live births

Life expectancy at birth: 70.01 years

Total fertility rate: 3.04 children born/woman

Ethnic Groups:

    Amerindian:45%

    Mestizo (mixed Amerindian and white): 37%

    White: 15%

    Other: 3%

Religion:

    Roman Catholic: 90%

    Other: 10%

Official languages: Spanish, Quechua

Literacy (definition: age 15 or over who can read and write):

    Total population: 88.7%

    Male: 94.5%

    Female: 83%

ECONOMY

Gross domestic product (GDP): $116 billion

GDP growth rate: 2.4%

GDP per capita: $4,400

GDP by sector:

    Agriculture: 13%

    Industry: 42%

    Services: 45%

Population below poverty line: 54%

Inflation rate: 5.5%

Labor force: 7.6 million

Unemployment rate: 7.7%

Budget:

    Revenues: $8.5 billion

    Expenditures: $9.3 billion

Industries: mining, petroleum, fishing, textiles, clothing, food processing, cement, auto assembly, steel, shipbuilding

Agricultural products: coffee, cotton, sugarcane, rice, wheat, potatoes,
coca, poultry, beef, dairy products, wool, fish

Exports: $5.9 billion

Imports: $8.4 billion

Currency: *nuevo sol* (3.5 *nuevo sol* per U.S. dollar in January 2000)

NOTES

INTRODUCTION: A PAUPER ON A THRONE OF GOLD

1. Rex A. Hudson, ed. *Peru: A Country Study.* Washington, DC: Library of Congress, Federal Research Division, 1993, p. 135.

2. Hudson, *Peru,* p. 135.

CHAPTER 1: THE MANY COLORS OF PERU

3. Pam Barrett, ed. *Insight Guide: Peru.* New York: Langenscheidt Publishers, 1999, p. 175.

4. Barrett, *Insight Guide: Peru,* p. 171.

5. Dilwyn Jenkins, *The Rough Guide to Peru.* New York: Penguin Putnam, 2000, p. 288.

6. Jane Holligan de Diaz-Limaco, *Peru in Focus: A Guide to the People, Politics, and Culture.* New York: Interlink Books, 1998, p. 10.

7. Quoted in Jenkins, *The Rough Guide to Peru,* p. 201.

8. Barrett, *Insight Guide: Peru,* p. 213.

9. Barrett, *Insight Guide: Peru,* p. 219.

10. Jenkins, *The Rough Guide to Peru,* p. 104.

CHAPTER 2: THE INCA AND INTRUDERS

11. Adriana van Hagen, "Lost Empires: Peru Before the Incas," *Insight Guide: Peru,* ed. Pam Barrett. New York: Langenscheidt Publishers, 1999, p. 27.

12. van Hagen, "Lost Empires: Peru Before the Incas," p. 30.

13. Brian Fagan, "The Chavin Cult," *The Peru Reader: History, Culture, Politics,* ed. Orin Starn et al. Durham, NC: Duke University Press, 1995, p. 20.

14. Fagan, "The Chavin Cult," p. 22.

15. van Hagen, "Lost Empires: Peru Before the Incas," p. 32.

16. Peter Frost, "The Incas," *Insight Guide: Peru,* p. 37.

17. Frost, "The Incas," p. 37.

18. Frost, "The Incas," p. 42.

19. Holligan de Diaz-Limaco, *Peru in Focus*, p. 22.

CHAPTER 3: FROM COLONY TO CONTEMPORARY NATION

20. Jenkins, *The Rough Guide to Peru*, p. 423.

21. Jenkins, *The Rough Guide to Peru*, p. 53.

22. Jenkins, *The Rough Guide to Peru*, p. 53.

23. Holligan de Diaz-Limaco, *Peru in Focus*, p. 25.

24. Jenkins, *The Rough Guide to Peru*, p. 429.

25. Jane Holligan, "Democracy and Crisis," in *Insight Guide: Peru*, p. 68.

26. Quoted in Starn, *The Peru Reader*, p. 7.

CHAPTER 4: DAILY LIFE IN PERU

27. Barrett, *Insight Guide: Peru*, p. 89.

28. Hudson, *Peru: A Country Study*, pp. 127–28.

29. Holligan de Diaz-Limaco, *Peru in Focus*, p. 62.

30. Holligan de Diaz-Limaco, *Peru in Focus*, p. 63.

31. Hudson, *Peru: A Country Study*, p. 112.

32. Hudson, *Peru: A Country Study*, p. 111.

CHAPTER 5: ARTS AND CULTURE IN PERU

33. Simon Broughton et al., eds., *World Music: The Rough Guide.* London: Rough Guides, 1995, p. 584.

34. *Music of the Andes.* Compact disc liner notes. London: World Music Network, 1996.

35. Broughton, *World Music*, p. 585.

36. Barrett, *Insight Guide: Peru*, p. 112.

37. Broughton, *World Music*, p. 589.

38. Broughton, *World Music*, p. 589.

39. Quoted in Broughton, *World Music*, p. 589.

40. Jenkins, *The Rough Guide to Peru*, p. 475.

41. Holligan de Diaz-Limaco, *Peru in Focus*, p. 79.

42. Jenkins, *The Rough Guide to Peru*, p. 475.

43. Quoted in Starn, *The Peru Reader*, p. 237.

CHAPTER 6: TOWARD A TRULY SHINING PATH: CHALLENGES OF CONTEMPORARY PERU

44. Hudson, *Peru: A Country Study*, p. 133.

45. Hudson, *Peru: A Country Study*, p. 4.

46. Hudson, *Peru: A Country Study*, p. 131.

47. Hudson, *Peru: A Country Study*, p. 170.

CHRONOLOGY

2500 B.C.
Peruvian coast inhabited by people living in small villages.

1800 B.C.
Initial Period; coastal inhabitants move inland, begin irrigating land.

800 B.C.
Chavín culture produces oldest known gold and silver objects.

300 B.C.–A.D. 600
Early Intermediate Period.

1000
Chachapoya and Chimu cultures emerge; city of Chan Chan built.

ca. 1400
Beginning of rise of Inca Empire.

1532
Atahualpa defeats Huáscar for control of the Inca Empire; Francisco Pizarro arrives in Peru.

1533
Atahualpa killed by Spanish.

1535
Pizarro founds city of Lima.

1541
Pizarro killed in Lima.

1570s
Encomienda system established.

1572
Tupac Amarú killed by Spanish.

1808
Napoléon unseats Spanish monarch, causing unrest in Latin America.

1821
Peru declares independence.

1824–27
Presidency of Simon Bolívar.

1827–65
Political chaos in Peru results in thirty-five changes in government.

1840–65
Guano boom.

1879–83
War of the Pacific between Peru, Chile, and Bolivia.

1880–1910
Rubber boom in Amazon.

1924
Víctor Raúl Haya de la Torre founds APRA (Alianza Popular Revolucionaria Americana).

1932
One thousand Apristas (APRA party members) killed at Chan Chan in retaliation for police deaths in a violent labor protest.

1963–68
Francisco Belaunde presidency.

1968
Quechua recognized as second official language.

1968–75
Juan Velasco presidency.

1977–80
Víctor Raúl Haya de la Torre presidency.

1980s
Sendero Luminoso (Shining Path) begins terrorist campaign in Peru.

1980–85
Second Belaunde presidency.

1983
Powerful El Niño devastates country.

1985–90
Alan Garcia presidency.

1990
Alberto Fujimori wins presidency.

1992
Fujimori "self-coup" dissolves parliament and gives president more power; Abimael Guzmán, leader of Shining Path, arrested.

1996
Inflation brought under control to 10 percent; Tupac Amaru begins siege of Japanese embassy.

1998
Repeat of devastating El Niño.

2000
Fujimori announces decision to step down from presidency in wake of scandal involving bribery by intelligence chief Vladimiro Montesinos.

GLOSSARY

archaeologist: Someone who studies ancient architectural sites.

basin: Low-lying region where runoff collects to form rivers.

ceja de selva: Edge, or "eyebrow," of the jungle.

charango: Small guitar used in traditional Andean music.

chicha: Beer brewed from corn; also a contemporary musical style.

cholo: One of the terms used for Indian; also a contemporary musical style.

conjunto: Musical group.

conquistador: Spanish term for conqueror.

cordillera: Mountain range.

costa: Coast.

criollo: Term loosely applied to Peruvians of European origin.

cumbia: Colombian dance style popular in Peru.

El Dorado: Fictional land of such wealth that cities are made of gold and gems.

encomendero: Holder of an *encomienda.*

encomienda: Colonial land grant including the labor of the Indians living on it.

extractive: Referring to technologies and practices that take products from the environment.

free trade: Policy of minimizing restrictions on imports and exports.

guano: Fertilizer obtained from bird droppings.

hacienda: Large estate.

huaquero: Someone who looks for *huacos,* or pre-Columbian artifacts.

huayno: A traditional Andean musical style.

indigenista: Writer focusing on the lives of indigenous Peruvians.

indigenous: Living naturally in a place rather than brought in from the outside.

mate: Popular herbal beverage.

mestizo: Term for a person of "mixed" Indian and Spanish blood.

metallurgist: Someone who studies and works with metals.

mita: Inca system of requiring communities to contribute labor for the good of the state.

montaña: Mountain.

nationalism: Attitude that one's country is of extreme importance.

nationalization: Process by which a government takes over privately owned industries.

plaza: Town square.

reducciónes: Communities formed in the colonial era by forcing Indians to relocate.

selva: Jungle.

Senderista: Member or supporter of Sendero Luminoso, or Shining Path, a terrorist organization.

shantytowns: Quickly constructed settlements of temporary housing, usually lacking basic amenities such as running water.

sierra: Mountains.

terrace: Ledge cut into a steep mountainside on which plants are cultivated.

SUGGESTIONS FOR FURTHER READING

Joan Abelove, *Go and Come Back*. New York: DK Inc., 1998. Young adult novel about the arrival of two anthropologists in an Amazon village and the culture clashes that ensue, told from the point of view of a teenage girl of the village.

David Getz, *Frozen Girl*. New York: Henry Holt, 1998. This account of the discovery of the mummified remains of a young girl sacrificed in the Andes centuries ago includes historical information as well as discussion of the significance of the find.

Pedro de Cieza de Leon, *The Discovery and Conquest of Peru: Chronicles of the New World Encounter*. Eds. Alexander Parma Cook and Noble David Cook. Durham, NC: Duke University Press, 1999. Excellent new translation of a contemporary account of Pizarro's conquest of Peru.

Emilie U. Lepthien, *Peru*. Chicago: Children's Press, 1992. This volume in the Enchantment of the World series provides very basic but clear information.

Elizabeth Mann, *Machu Picchu: The Story of the Amazing Inkas and Their City in the Clouds*. New York: Mikaya Press, 2000. Written for young adult readers, this book tells the story of the creation and use of Machu Picchu.

Susan Vande Griek, *A Gift for Ampato*. Toronto, Ontario, Canada: Groundwork Books/Douglas & McIntyre, 1999. A fictional version of the recently discovered mummy girl's life and death.

WORKS CONSULTED

BOOKS

Anthony F. Aveni, *Between the Lines: The Mystery of the Giant Ground Drawings of Ancient Nazca, Peru*. Austin: University of Texas Press, 2000. Interesting, well-illustrated work laying out and analyzing theories about the Nazca Lines.

Pam Barrett, Ed., *Insight Guide: Peru*. New York: Langenscheidt Publishers, 1999. This volume in the Insight Guide series provides excellent information and contains informative photographs and sidebars.

Simon Broughton et al., Eds., *World Music: The Rough Guide*. London: Rough Guides, 1995.

Nigel Davies, *The Ancient Kingdoms of Peru*. New York: Penguin, 1998. Thorough, scholarly work on Peru before the conquest.

Gustavo Gorriti Ellenbogen, *The Shining Path: A History of the Millenarian War in Peru*. Trans. Robin Kirk. Durham: University of North Carolina Press, 1999. Important work by a renowned Peruvian historian.

Brian Fagan, "The Chavin Cult," in *The Peru Reader*. Eds. Starn, Degregori, and Kirk.

Peter Frost, "The Incas," in *Insight Guide: Peru*.

Adriana van Hagen, "Lost Empires: Peru Before the Incas," in *Insight Guide: Peru*.

Jane Holligan, "Democracy and Crisis," in *Insight Guide: Peru*.

Jane Holligan de Diaz-Limaco, *Peru in Focus: A Guide to the People, Politics, and Culture*. New York: Interlink Books, 1998. Provides good summary information on a wide range of topics.

Rex A. Hudson, Ed., *Peru: A Country Study*. Washington, DC: Library of Congress, Federal Research Division, 1993. One in a series of country studies used by diplomats and others as background material on history, current events, the economy, and other subjects.

Dilwyn Jenkins, *The Rough Guide to Peru*. New York: Penguin Putnam, 2000. One in a series of *Rough Guides*, this book contains excellent background information as well as travel information for tourists.

Cynthia McClintock, *Revolutionary Movements in Latin America*. Washington, DC: United States Institute of Peace Press, 1998. This acclaimed work focuses extensively on Sendero Luminoso.

Kenneth M. Roberts, *Deepening Democracy? The Modern Left and Social Movement in Chile and Peru*. Stanford CA: Stanford University Press, 1999. Scholarly discussion of the current political situation in Peru.

Orin Starn, Carlos Ivan Degregori, and Robin Kirk, eds., *The Peru Reader: History, Culture, Politics*. Durham, NC: Duke University Press, 1995. This anthology of articles about Peru's past, present, and future is very thorough and well written. Also contains selections from the works of Peruvian poets and other writers.

Susan C. Stokes, *Cultures in Conflict: Social Movement and the State in Peru*. Berkeley: University of California Press, 1995. Contains interviews, observations by the author, and surveys to provide insight into shantytown life in Peru.

WEBSITES

CIA: The World Factbook 2000. www.odci.gov/cia/publications/factbook/geos/pe.html. Provides updates of information in *Peru: A Country Study*.

MSNBC: www.msnbc.com. Good source of up-to-date news on a wide variety of subjects.

Salon.com News: www.salon.com. Features in-depth articles on current events.

OTHER

Music of the Andes. Compact disc liner notes. London: World Music Network, 1996.

INDEX

Picture Credits

About the Author

Laurel Corona lives in Lake Arrowhead, California, and teaches English and humanities at San Diego City College. She has a master's degree from the University of Chicago and a Ph.D. from the University of California at Davis. Dr. Corona has written many other books for Lucent Books including *Brazil*, *Ethiopia*, *Norway*, *Life in Moscow*, *The Russian Federation*, and *Ukraine*.